Nuts

JOKE BOOK

THIS IS A CARLTON BOOK

Published by The Carlton Publishing Group
20 Mortimer Street
London W1T 3JW

ISBN: 978-1-84442-142-8

10 9 8 7 6 5
Printed in Great Britain

Nuts

JOKE BOOK

CARLTON

A message from THE *Nuts* TEAM

If I should happen to make any spelling mistakes in this opening message, it's because I am trying to write it in the middle of a laughing fit. A fit caused by the merest glance I have taken at the contents of the very book you now hold in your hand. I can't stop. It's the jokes, you see! The fantastic avalanche of jokes!

When it comes to jokes, we like to think that we at *Nuts* magazine bring you the very best – and occasionally rudest – every week. In fact, we think that we are so good at the gathering of hilarious gags that we have decided to prove it, by giving to the world the very first *Nuts Joke Book*. In its chortle-stuffed pages you'll find literally hundreds of one-liners, puns, shaggy dog stories and episodes in which unlikely animals walk into pubs – all of them hand-picked from the Jokes page of *Nuts*. Which means all of these jokes were actually told by YOU, the *Nuts* reader. Which technically makes you an author now. Congratulations!

And so I invite you to enjoy the joke book you helped to write. But if you laugh so hard your brain explodes, don't blame us.

In a hole

A man loved golf, but his eyesight was so bad he couldn't find his ball once he'd hit it. His wife recommended he take along her uncle, Ted.

The golfer said, "But Ted's 80 years old and half-senile!"

His wife replied, "Yes, but his eyesight's incredible."

So the man agreed to take Ted along. He teed off and could feel that he'd hit it solidly. He asked Ted, "Do you see it?"

Ted nodded his head and said, "Boy, that was a beautiful shot!"

The man excitedly asked, "Well, where did it land?!"

Ted said, "Um... I forget."

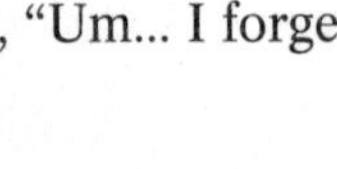

Grave concern

A man, his wife and his mother-in-law went on holiday to Jerusalem. While they were there, the mother-in-law passed away. The undertaker told them, "You can have her shipped home for £5,000, or you can bury her here in the Holy Land for £150."

The man thought about it and told him he'd just have her shipped home. The undertaker asked, "Why would you spend £5,000 to ship your mother-in-law home when it would be wonderful for her to be buried here and you would spend only £150?" The man replied, "Long ago a man died here, was buried here, and three days later he rose from the dead. I just can't take that chance."

How do you tell if a redneck's married?
There are tobacco-spit stains on both sides of the truck.

Better shape up

After passing his driving test, Davey comes home and says, "Dad, can I use the car?"

His dad replies, "OK, son, but first you have to mow the lawn every week for three months and get your hair cut."

Three months pass and Davey comes into the house and says, "Dad, the lawn's looked like Lords for the last three months. How about letting me use the car now?"

The dad replies, "That's true. But, son, you didn't cut your hair."

So Davey says, "But, Dad, Jesus had long hair!"

"You're right," says Davey's dad. "And he walked everywhere."

If it works for you...

A woman spots a little old man sitting happily on a park bench and wanders over for a chat.

"I can't help but notice how happy you look," she says. "What's your secret?"

"Well," replies the man, "I smoke, drink, eat junk food all day and don't exercise..."

"Wow!" replies the woman. "How old are you?"

"Twenty-three."

Little short of a miracle

A man goes into a shop and sees something he doesn't recognise. He asks the assistant what it is. The assistant replies, "That's a Thermos flask. It keeps hot things hot and cold things cold."

Amazed by this incredible invention, the man buys it immediately.

He walks into work the next day with his new Thermos. His boss sees him and asks, "What's that shiny object?"

"It keeps hot things hot and cold things cold," says the man, proudly.

The boss asks, "What do you have in it?"

"Two cups of tea and some ice-cream," the man replies.

That's my girl

Bruce is driving over the Sydney Harbour Bridge one day when he sees his girlfriend, Sheila, about to throw herself off.

Bruce slams on the brakes and yells, "Sheila, what the hell d'ya think you're doing?"

Sheila turns around with a tear in her eye and says, "G'day, Bruce. Ya got me pregnant and so now I'm gonna kill meself."

Bruce gets a lump in his throat when he hears this. "Strewth, Sheila. Not only are you a great shag, but you're a real sport, too!"

Properly shafted

An agent finds out that his top actress client has been moonlighting as an escort. Having long lusted after her, he asks if he can have sex with her later that night. She agrees, but says, "You'll have to pay like everyone else."

The agent agrees and meets the actress at her house that night. After turning out all the lights, they have sex. The actress falls asleep, but ten minutes later, she is awoken and the scene repeats itself. This goes on for the next few hours.

Eventually, the actress screams out, "This is amazing! I never knew agents were so virile."

A voice from the dark replies, "Lady, I'm not your agent. He's at the door selling tickets."

Sick as a parrot

Raul, Ronaldo and Beckham were all in Real Madrid's canteen, eating their packed lunches. Raul looked at his and said, "Tapas again! If I get tapas one more time, I'm jumping off the top of the Bernabeu."

Ronaldo opened his lunchbox and exclaimed, "Burritos! If I get burritos again, I'll do the same."

Beckham opened his lunchbox and said, "Ham and cheese again. If I get a ham and cheese sandwich one more time, I'm jumping too."

The next day, Raul opened his lunchbox, saw some tapas and jumped to his death. Then Ronaldo opened his lunchbox, saw a burrito and jumped too.

Finally, Beckham opened his lunchbox, saw some ham and cheese sandwiches and followed the others in a fatal plunge.

At the funeral, Raul's wife was weeping. She said, "If I'd known how tired he was of tapas, I never would have given it to him again."

Ronaldo's wife also wept and said, "I could have given him tacos or enchiladas! I didn't realise he hated burritos so much."

Everyone turned to Victoria Beckham, dressed in black Versace.

"Hey, don't look at me," said Posh. "David made his own lunch."

What happens to someone fired from a job at a fairground?
They sue for funfair dismissal.

How to handle a woman

After hearing a couple's complaints that their sex life wasn't what it used to be, a sex counsellor suggests they try the wheelbarrow position. They go home and the husband is raring to go. "Well, OK," the hesitant wife agrees, "but only on one condition; you have to promise me that we won't go past my parents' house."

Bottoms up

One day, a French spy received a coded message from a British MI6 agent. It read: S370HSSV-0773H.

The spy was stumped, so he sent it to his similarly clueless boss, who forwarded it to Russia.

The Russians couldn't solve it either, so they asked the Germans.

The Germans, having received this same message during WWII from the Brits, suggested turning it upside down.

The capital of America

A girl goes into the doctor's office for a check-up. As she takes off her blouse, the doctor notices a red 'H' on her chest. "How did you get that mark?" asks the doctor. "Oh, my boyfriend went to Harvard and he's so proud of it he never takes off his Harvard sweatshirt, even when we make love," she replies.

A couple of days later, another girl comes in. As she takes off her blouse, the doctor notices a blue 'Y' on her chest. "My boyfriend went to Yale," explains the girl, "and he's so proud of it he never takes off his Yale sweatshirt, even when we make love."

A couple of days later, another girl comes in. She takes off her blouse to reveal a green 'M' on her chest. "Do you have a boyfriend at Michigan?" asks the doctor.

"No, but I have a girlfriend at Wisconsin. Why do you ask?"

Two chimps in a bath. One says, "Oh, oh, ah, ah, ee, ee!"
The other one says, "Put some cold water in then."

Swamp thing

A man walks into a pub with his dog on a lead.

The landlord says, “That’s a weird-looking dog. He’s got stumpy legs, he’s pink and he doesn’t have a tail. I bet my rottweiler could beat him in a scrap.” They bet £50 and, out in the backyard, the rottweiler is soon whimpering for mercy.

Another drinker says his pit bull will win and the bet is increased to £100. Another trip to the backyard, and when it’s all over the pitbull is cowering behind his owner, who pays up and says, “So what breed is he, anyway?”

The owner says, “Well, until I cut his tail off and painted him pink, he was the same breed as every other alligator.”

Mission of mercy

A surgeon was relaxing on his sofa one evening when the phone rang. The doctor calmly answered it and heard the familiar voice of a colleague on the other end of the line. “We need a fourth for poker,” said the friend.

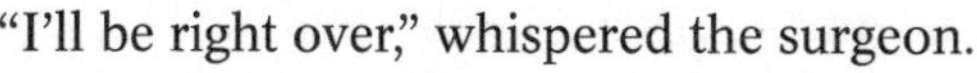

“I’ll be right over,” whispered the surgeon.

As he was putting on his coat, his wife asked, “Is it serious?”

“Oh, yes, quite serious,” said the surgeon, gravely. “Three doctors are there already!”

Forget I mentioned it

A bloke is in a queue at the supermarket when he notices that the dishy blonde behind him has raised her hand and is smiling at him.

He is rather taken aback that such a looker would be waving to him and, although she's familiar, he can't place where he knows her from, so he says, "Sorry, do you know me?"

She replies, "I may be mistaken, but I think you might be the father of one of my children."

His mind shoots back to the one and only time he has been unfaithful. "Christ!" he says. "Are you that strippergram on my stag night that I shagged on the snooker table in front of all my mates?"

"No," she replies. "I'm your son's English teacher."

Good for the roses

An American tourist in Dublin decides to duck out of his tour group and explore the city on his own. He wanders around, taking in the sights and occasionally stopping at a quaint pub to soak up the local culture, chat with the lads and have a pint of Guinness. After a while, he finds himself in a very high-class area: big, stately residences, no pubs, no shops, no restaurants and, worst of all, no public toilets. He really needs to go after all those pints of Guinness and manages to find a narrow side-street – the perfect solution to his problem. As he's unzipping, he's tapped on the shoulder by a policeman, who says, "I say, sir, you simply cannot do that here, you know."

"I'm very sorry, officer," replies the American, "but I really, really have to go and I just can't find a public toilet."

"Ah, yes," says the policeman. "Just follow me."

He leads him to a back delivery alley, then along a wall to a gate, which he opens. "In there," points the policeman. "Whizz away, sir. Anywhere you want." The fellow enters and finds himself in the most beautiful garden he has ever seen: manicured grass lawns, statues, fountains, sculptured hedges and huge beds of gorgeous flowers, all in perfect bloom. Since he has the policeman's blessing, he unburdens himself and is greatly relieved. As he goes back through the gate, he says to the policeman, "That was really decent of you. Is that your famed Irish hospitality?"

"No, sir," replies the cop. "That's what we call the British Embassy."

What do Kermit the Frog and Henry the Eighth have in common?
They both have the same middle name.

Meat is murder

A family was given some venison by a friend. The wife cooked up the deer steaks and served them to the husband and children.

The husband thought it would be fun to have his son guess what it was that they were eating.

"Is it beef?" little Eddie asked.

"No. I'll give you a clue," the dad said. "It's what your mum sometimes calls me."

"Is it useless, pathetic loser?" said Eddie.

The human condition

Two Arabs boarded a flight out of London. One took a window seat and the other sat next to him in the middle seat.

Just before take-off, an American sat down in the aisle seat. After take-off, the American kicked his shoes off and was settling in for the flight when the Arab in the window seat said, "Excuse me. I need to get up and get a Coke."

"Don't get up," said the American, "I'm in the aisle seat. I'll get it for you."

As soon as he left, one of the Arabs picked up the American's right shoe and spat in it.

When the American returned with the Coke, the other Arab said, "That looks good; I'd really like one, too."

The American went to fetch it and, while he was gone, the

other Arab picked up his left shoe and spat in it.

Once the American returned with the drink, they all sat back and enjoyed the flight.

As the plane was landing, the American slipped his feet into his shoes and knew immediately what had happened.

"Why does it have to be this way?" the American asked out loud. "How long must this go on?"

He turned to look at the two Arabs. "All this distrust between our great nations? All this hatred? All this animosity? All this spitting in shoes and pissing in Cokes?"

Sole man

A lady goes into a bar and sees a cowboy with his feet propped up on a table. He has the biggest feet she's ever seen. The woman asks the cowboy if what they say about men with big feet is true.

The cowboy replies, "Sure is. Why don't you come back to my place and let me prove it?"

The woman spends the night with him. The next day, she hands the cowboy a hundred dollars.

Blushing, he says, "I'm flattered; nobody has ever paid me for my prowess before."

The woman replies, "Well, don't be. Take this money and go buy yourself some boots that fit!"

Number-crunching

Donald Rumsfeld is giving the President his daily briefing on Iraq. He concludes by saying: "Yesterday, seven Brazilian soldiers were killed in an ambush."

"Oh, no! That's terrible!" the President exclaims.

His staff sit stunned at this display of emotion, nervously watching as the President sits, head in hands.

Finally, the President looks up and asks, "Um... how many is a brazillion, exactly?"

Why are pirates called pirates?
They just arrrr!

Death from above

A woman walks into the kitchen to find her husband stalking around with a fly-swatter.

"What are you doing?" she asks.

"Hunting flies," he replies.

"Oh. Killed any?" she enquires.

"Three males and two females," the husband responds.

Intrigued, she asks, "How can you tell?"

"Easy," the husband replies. "Three were on a beer can and the other two were on the phone."

Older is better

Over dinner with the chairman of Ford, Bill Gates starts boasting. "If automotive technology had kept up with computer technology over the past few decades," says Gates, "you could now be driving a V-32 instead of a V-8, and it would have a top speed of 10,000 miles per hour: or you could have an economy car that weighs 30 pounds and gets a thousand miles to a gallon of gas."

"Sure," says the Ford chairman. "But who'd want a car that crashes four times a day?"

Holey cow

A farmer is helping a cow give birth when he notices his four-year-old son standing wide-eyed at the fence, witnessing the entire thing.

"Dammit," the man says to himself. "Now I'm going to have to explain about the birds and the bees." Not wanting to jump the gun, the man decides to wait and see if his son asks any questions.

After everything is finished, he walks over to his lad and asks, "Well, son, do you have any questions?"

"Just one," the child says. "How fast was the calf going when it hit that cow?"

You had to be there

Three old men were drinking around a pub table. At the table next to them sat a young girl.

The first man said, “I think it’s spelt w-o-o-m-b.” And the second replied, “No, it must be w-o-o-o-m-b-h.” The third said, “No, no, you both have it wrong – it’s w-o-o-m.”

At this, the young lady could stand it no longer. She got up and said, “It’s spelt w-o-m-b, you fools.”

“Listen, love,” said one of the old men. “Have you even heard an elephant fart underwater?”

That’s telling her

Little Tommy is sitting on a park bench, stuffing a bag of pick-and-mix into his mouth, when an old lady comes over to tell him off. “Son, don’t you know that eating all those sweets will rot your teeth and make you sick?”

“My grandfather lived to be 105 years old!” replies Tommy.

“Did he always eat a whole bag of sweets in one go?” the old lady retorts.

“No,” answers Tommy, “but he did mind his own business.”

And I think to myself... what a waterfowl world

Three women die together in an accident and go to Heaven. When they get there, Saint Peter says, "We only have one rule here in Heaven; don't step on the ducks."

Sure enough, there are ducks everywhere in Heaven. It is almost impossible not to step on a duck and, although they try their best to avoid them, the first woman accidentally steps on one. Along comes Saint Peter with the ugliest man she ever saw.

Saint Peter chains them together and says, "Your punishment for stepping on a duck is to spend eternity chained to this ugly man."

The next day, the second woman steps on a duck and along comes Saint Peter. With him is another extremely ugly man. He chains them together with the same admonition as he gave the first woman.

The third woman, having observed all this, is very, very careful where she steps. She manages to go months without stepping on any ducks, but one day Saint Peter comes up to her with the most handsome man she's ever seen and, silently, he chains them together. The happy woman says, "Wonder what I did to deserve being chained to you for all of eternity?"

The guy says, "I don't know about you, but I stepped on a duck."

A boy goes to the Jobcentre and says, "I'd like to work in a bowling alley." "Ten pin?" says the man behind the desk. "No, permanent," says the boy.

The cruel sea

The first mate on a ship decided to celebrate his birthday with some contraband rum. Unfortunately, he was still drunk the next morning. Realising this, the captain wrote in the ship's log: "The first mate was drunk today."

"Captain, please don't let that stay in the log," the mate said. "This could add months or years to my becoming a captain myself."

"Is it true?" asked the captain, already knowing the answer.

"Yes, it's true," the mate said.

"Then, if it's true, it has to go in the log. That's the rule," said the captain, sternly.

A few weeks later, it was the first mate's turn to make the log entries. The first mate wrote: "The ship seems in particularly good shape. The captain was sober today."

Oopsy!

While attending a convention, three psychiatrists take a walk. "People are always coming to us with their guilt and fears," one says, "but we have no one to go to with our problems. Since we're all professionals, why don't we listen to each other?"

The first psychiatrist confesses, "I'm a compulsive gambler and deeply in debt, so I overcharge patients as often as I can."

The second admits, "I have a drug problem that's out of control, and I frequently pressure my patients into buying illegal drugs for me."

The third psychiatrist says, "I just can't keep a secret."

Baggage allowance

Dave says to Phil, "You know, I reckon I'm about ready for a holiday, only this year I'm gonna do it a little different. The last few years, I took your advice as to where to go. Two years ago you said to go to Tenerife; I went to Tenerife, and Marie got pregnant. Then last year you told me to go to the Bahamas; I went to the Bahamas, and Marie got pregnant again."

Phil says, "So what are you gonna do different this year?"

Dave says, "This year, I'm takin' Marie with me..."

Snot a problem

A man and a woman are sitting next to one another on a flight to New York. The woman sneezes, takes out a tissue, wipes her nose and then shudders for about ten seconds. A few minutes later, the woman sneezes again. Once more, she takes a tissue, wipes her nose and then shudders. A few more minutes pass before the woman sneezes and shudders again. Curious, the man says, "I can't help noticing that you keep sneezing and shuddering. Are you OK?"

"I'm so sorry if I disturbed you," says the woman. "I suffer from a condition that means whenever I sneeze, I have an orgasm."

"My God!" says the man. "Are you taking anything for it?"

"Yes," says the woman. "Pepper."

Present laughter

Four brothers grow up to become wealthy doctors and lawyers. At a meal, they're discussing what gifts they're about to give their elderly mother for her birthday. The first brother pipes up, "I've had a big house built for her."

Another sibling chips in with, "Well, I've had a £100,000 cinema installed in that house for her."

"That's nothing," offers the third brother. "I had my car dealer deliver her a brand-new Ferrari Enzo."

The remaining brother finally speaks up: "You know how

Mum loved reading the Bible, but she can't read so well these days? Well, I met this priest who has a parrot that recites the entire book! It took 12 years to teach him – and I've had to pledge to contribute £100,000 to the Church – but I've got him! Mum just has to name the chapter and verse and the parrot will recite it." The brothers are impressed.

Post-birthday, Mum pens some thank-you notes. "David, the house you built is so huge! I live in only one room, but I have to clean the whole place! Not great, but thanks anyway, son." To her second eldest she writes: "Michael, that cinema holds 50 people... but all my friends are dead! I'll never use it. Thank you for the gesture all the same." "Peter," she writes to her third eldest, "I'm too old to drive, so I never use the Enzo. The thought was kind. Thanks."

Finally, the youngest boy receives his letter: "Dearest Richard! You were the only son to have the good sense to put a little thought into your gift. The chicken was absolutely delicious!"

What did the elephant say to the naked man?
It's cute, but can you pick up peanuts with it?

Pier pressure

Every morning a man took the ferry to work. One morning, he woke up and found he had no electricity. He had no idea what time it was, but assumed he was late since he had a tendency to sleep late anyway.

So he scoffed down his breakfast, rushed to the port where he saw the ferry ten feet from the dock, and took a running leap. He barely made it, skidding across the deck of the boat, and hurt himself quite badly. "You know," said the captain, "in another minute we would have docked."

Struck down in his prime

A man tells his doctor he's unable to do all the things round the house that he used to. After an examination, he says, "Tell me in plain English what's wrong with me, Doc."

"Well, in layman's terms, you're lazy," says the doctor.

"OK. Now give me a medical term, so I can tell my wife."

Animal magnetism

An Aussie walks into his bedroom with a sheep under his arm and says: "Darling, this is the pig I have sex with when you have a headache."

His girlfriend, lying in bed, says: "I think you'll find that's a sheep."

The man replies: "I think you'll find I wasn't talking to you."

Cometh the hour, cometh the man

A fire starts inside a chemical plant and the alarm goes out to fire stations miles around. After crews have been fighting the fire for more than an hour, the chemical company president approaches the fire chief and says, "All our secret formulae are in the vault. They must be saved. I'll give £100,000 to the firemen who bring them out safely." Suddenly, another engine comes roaring down the road and drives straight into the middle of the inferno. The other men watch, unbelieving, as the firemen hop off their engine and heroically extinguish the fire, saving the secret formulae. The company president walks over to reward the volunteers and asks them, "What do you fellas plan to do with the money?" The driver looks him right in the eye and answers, "Well, the first thing we're going to do is fix the brakes."

Johnny was in class when the teacher farted. Embarrassed, she said, "Johnny, stop that!" To which Johnny replied, "Which way did it go, Miss?"

Now spit

A man and a woman meet at a bar. They get along so well that they decide to go to the woman's house. A few drinks later, the man takes off his shirt and then washes his hands. He then takes off his trousers and washes his hands again. The woman has been watching him and says, "You must be a dentist." The man, surprised, says, "Yes! How did you work that out?" "Easy," she replied, "you keep washing your hands." One thing leads to another and they make love. After, the woman says, "You must be a good dentist." The man, now with boosted ego, asks, "Sure, but how did you work it out?" The woman replies, "I didn't feel a thing."

It was worth a try

A mild-mannered man is tired of his wife always bossing him around, so he decides to be more assertive.

When he gets home from work, he says to his wife, "From now on, I'm the man of this house. When I come home from work, I want my dinner on the table. Now go upstairs and lay me some clothes on the bed, because I'm going out with the boys tonight. Then draw my bath. And, when I get out of the tub, guess who's going to dress me?"

"The undertaker?" she replies.

It's a tuft job, but someone's got to do it

A bloke goes into the Jobcentre in London and spots a job vacancy which reads, "Wanted: single man, willing to travel, must have own scissors. £500 a week guaranteed, plus company car and all expenses."

It sounds a bit too good to be true, so the bloke fronts up at the counter and quotes the job's reference number.

"Oh, that one," says the clerk. "It's a modelling agency here in London. They're looking for a pubic hair snipper. They supply girls who model underwear and before they go on the catwalk they report to you to snip off any wisps of pubic hair that are showing. It pays well, but there are drawbacks; it involves a lot of travel to exotic places and you have to get used to living in first-class hotels."

"Well, I'd still like to apply," says the bloke.

The clerk says, "OK, here's an application form and a rail ticket to Manchester."

"What do I wanna go to Manchester for?"

"Well," says the clerk, "that's where the end of the queue is at the moment."

What did the sign on the brothel door say?
We're closed. Beat it!

Epic journey

After a DIY store sponsored Ellen Macarthur's solo sea voyage, a man went into the store to congratulate them. "Well done for getting a yacht to leave the UK on November 28, 2004, sail 27,354 miles around the world and arrive back 72 days later," said the man. "Absolutely amazing."

"Well, thank you," replied the startled employee.

"Now, is there any chance you could let me know when the kitchen I ordered 96 days ago will be delivered from your warehouse 13 miles away?"

What's the difference between a mechanic and a herd of elephants?
The mechanic charges more.

Eugh!

A cowboy and an Indian are riding their horses together when they both stop and jump down. The Indian lies flat on the floor and puts his ear to the ground.

"Buffalo come!" cries the Indian.

"How do you know that?" asks the cowboy, impressed.

"Easy: ear stuck to ground," the Indian replies.

Body language

BB King's wife wants to surprise him for his birthday, so she goes to a tattoo parlour and has a big 'B' tattooed on each of her buttocks.

When BB gets home later that night, he opens the door to find his wife naked and bent over showing off her new tattoos. BB can't believe his eyes and screams, "Who the hell's Bob?"

Scrotal recall

A man is lying in bed in the hospital with an oxygen mask over his mouth. A young nurse appears to sponge his hands and feet.

"Excuse me, nurse," he mumbles from behind the mask, "Are my testicles black?"

Embarrassed, the young nurse replies, "I don't know; I'm only here to give you a bed-bath."

He struggles again to ask, "Nurse, are my testicles black?"

Finally, she pulls back the covers, raises his gown, holds his penis in one hand and his testicles in her other hand and takes a close look, and says, "There's nothing wrong with them."

Finally, the man pulls off his oxygen mask and replies, "That was very nice, but are... my... test... results... back?"

The majesty of the law

After listening to an elderly prostitute plead her case, Judge Poe calls a brief recess and retires to his chambers. En route, he bumps into a colleague, Judge Graham.

"Excuse me, Judge Graham," Poe asks. "What would you give a 63-year-old prostitute?"

"Let me think," Judge Graham replies. "Ten quid, tops."

Braking the habit

One day, a mechanic was working under a car when some brake fluid accidentally dripped into his mouth. "Wow," said the mechanic to himself. "That stuff tastes good."

The following day, he told his mate about his discovery. "It tastes great," said the mechanic. "I think I'll try a little more today."

The next day, the mechanic told his mate he'd drunk a pint of the stuff. His friend was worried but didn't say anything until the next day, when the mechanic revealed he'd drunk two pints.

"Don't you know that brake fluid is toxic? It's really bad for you," said his mate.

"I know what I'm doing," snapped the mechanic. "I can stop any time I want to."

Vow of silence

A mafia godfather finds out that his bookkeeper has swindled him out of ten million dollars. This bookkeeper is deaf, so the godfather brings along his attorney, who knows sign language.

The godfather asks the bookkeeper, "Where's the ten million you embezzled from me?"

The attorney, using sign language, asks the bookkeeper where the money is hidden.

The bookkeeper signs, "I don't know what you're talking about."

The attorney tells the godfather: "He says he doesn't know what you're talking about."

At this point, the godfather pulls out a 9mm pistol, puts it to the bookkeeper's temple, cocks it and says, "Ask him again!"

"He'll kill you if you don't talk," signs the attorney.

The bookkeeper signs back: "OK. You win! The money is buried in my cousin Enzo's back yard."

The godfather asks the attorney, "Well, what'd he say?"

The attorney replies, "He says you don't have the balls..."

Legend in his own lifetime

An artist asks a gallery-owner if there's been any interest in his paintings recently.

"I have good news and bad news," the gallery owner tells him. "The good news is a gentleman enquired about your work and wondered if it would appreciate in value after your death. When I told him it would, he bought all 15 of your paintings."

"That's great," the artist says. "What's the bad news?"

"He was your doctor."

Why is Tottenham Hotspur a bit like Kim Wilde?
Glamorous in the Eighties, but not so nice to watch now.

Calls from mobiles may cost more

Several men are in the changing room of a golf club when a mobile phone on a bench rings and a man answers. He switches to hands-free and everyone else in the room stops to listen.

"Hello," says the guy.

A female voice answers, "Honey, it's me. Are you at the club?"

"Yes," replies the man.

"I'm at the shops now and found this beautiful leather coat. It's only £1,000. Is it OK if I buy it?"

"Sure, go ahead if you like it that much," says the guy, nonchalantly.

The woman goes on. "I also stopped by the Mercedes garage and saw the new models. I saw one I really liked."

"How much?" enquires the man.

"£60,000," says the spendthrift.

"OK, but for that price I want it with all the options," says the fella.

"Great!" says the woman. "Oh, and one more thing. The house we wanted last year is back on the market. They're asking £950,000."

"Well, then go ahead and give them an offer, but just offer £900,000," replies the man.

"OK. I'll see you later! I love you!" the woman signs off.

"Bye, I love you, too," says the man and hangs up.

The other men in the changing room look at him in astonishment.

Then the man asks: "Anyone know whose phone this is?"

Every home should have one

A man walks into a pub with a small doll in his hand and says to the barmaid, “What’s this?”

He then pokes the doll in the stomach and a man in the corner of the pub screams. Without saying a word, the man then leaves.

The next day, the man walks back in the pub at the same time, and says to the same barmaid, “What’s this?”

He pokes the doll in the stomach as before and, once again, a man in the corner screams.

As the man is about to leave again, the barmaid shouts, “I don’t know. What is it?”

“Déja voodoo,” replies the man.

Why, you little...

A guy is driving down the road at 100mph singing, “Twenty-one today, twenty-one today!” Soon, a cop pulls him over and says, “Because it’s your birthday, I’ll let you off.”

Despite the cop’s warning, the guy screeches off and is soon doing a ton down the road again. The cop, in hot pursuit, then sees the man mow down a traffic warden. Suddenly, the man starts singing, “Twenty-two today, twenty-two today!”

How did Tarzan end up dying?
Picking cherries.

Tales from the crypt

Late one night, a young chap was walking home from a club. Most of the streetlights in the area were broken. Suddenly, he heard a strange noise. Startled, he turned and saw a coffin following him. He started to jog, but he heard the coffin speed up after him. Eventually, he made it to his front door, but he knew the coffin was only seconds behind. He dived inside, slamming the front door behind him.

Suddenly, there was a crash as the coffin smashed its way through the front door. In horror, the young lad fled upstairs to the bathroom and locked the door.

With an almighty smash, the bathroom door flew off its hinges and the coffin stood in its place.

Desperate, the young man reached into his bathroom cabinet. He grabbed a bar of Imperial Leather soap and threw it at the coffin, but still it came. He grabbed a can of Lynx deodorant and threw it, but still it came. Finally, he threw some cough mixture.

The coffin stopped.

Why do gorillas have red balls?
So they can hide in cherry trees.

What's round and snarling?
A vicious circle.

Beggars can't be choosers

Two friends were playing golf when one pulled out a cigar. He didn't have a lighter, so he asked his friend if he had one.

"Yep," he replied and pulled out a 12-inch Bic lighter from his golf bag.

"Wow!" said his friend. "Where did you get that monster?"

"I got it from the genie in my golf bag."

"You have a genie? Could I see him?"

The other bloke opens his golf bag and out pops a genie. The friend asks the genie, "Since I'm a friend of your master, will you grant me one wish?"

"Yes, I will," the genie replies. The friend asks the genie for a million bucks and the genie hops back into the golf bag and leaves him standing there, waiting for his million bucks. Suddenly, the sky darkens and the sound of a million ducks flying overhead is heard.

The friend tells his golfing partner, "I asked for a million bucks, not a million ducks!"

He answers, "I forgot to say; he's a bit deaf. Do you really think I asked him for a 12-inch Bic?"

A night to remember

As Claude the hypnotist took to the stage, he announced, "Unlike most stage hypnotists, I intend to hypnotise each and every member of the audience."

Claude then withdrew a beautiful antique pocket watch from his coat. "I want you each to keep your eye on this antique watch. It's a very special watch. It has been in my family for six generations."

He began to swing the watch gently back and forth while quietly chanting, "Watch the watch. Watch the watch. Watch the watch. Watch the watch. Watch the watch..."

Hundreds of pairs of eyes followed the swaying watch – until, unexpectedly, it slipped from Claude's fingers and fell to the floor, breaking into a hundred pieces.

"Sh*t!" exclaimed the hypnotist, loudly.

It took three weeks to clean the seats.

Why don't men fake orgasms?
Because no man would pull those faces on purpose.

Fair question

The instructor at a pregnancy and labour class is teaching the young couples how to breathe properly during delivery. The teacher announces, “Ladies, exercise is good for you. Walking is especially beneficial. And, gentlemen, it wouldn’t hurt you to take the time to go walking with your partner.” The room falls quiet. Finally, a man in the middle of the group raises his hand.

“Is it all right if she carries a golf bag while we walk?”

You’re in

A little old lady decides she wants to join a bikers’ club, so she goes to a meeting of the local Hells Angels. A big, bearded, leather-clad biker opens the door and asks what she wants.

“I want to join your club,” she tells him. Deciding to humour her, he asks if she has a bike. “Over there, in the car park,” she replies, pointing to a shiny new Harley.

“And do you drink?” he asks.

“Like a fish,” she says. “I can drink any bloke under the table.” The biker is now suitably impressed.

“OK,” he asks. “But have you ever been picked up by the fuzz?”

“No!” comes the reply. “But I have been swung around by the nipples a few times.”

All passion spent

One misty Scottish morning a man is driving down from Wick to Inverness. Suddenly, a huge red-haired highlander steps into the middle of the road. At the roadside there also stands a beautiful woman. The driver's attention is dragged from the girl when the highlander opens the car door and drags him from the seat.

"Right, you," he shouts. "I want you to masturbate."

"But..." stammers the driver.

"Now, or I'll bloody kill you!"

So the driver starts to masturbate. Thinking of the girl at the roadside, this only takes a few seconds.

"Right," says the highlander, "do it again!"

"But..." says the driver.

"Now!" shouts the highlander.

So the driver does it again.

This goes on for two hours until, finally, the driver collapses in an exhausted heap.

"Again!" says the highlander.

"I can't," whimpers the man. "You'll just have to kill me."

The highlander looks down at the man slumped on the roadside.

"All right," he says, "now you can give my daughter a lift to Inverness."

Not so sweet

A Jelly Baby goes to the doctor. "Doctor, doctor; I think I've got an STD."

The doctor is surprised, "You can't have an STD, you're a Jelly Baby!"

"But, doctor, I've been sleeping with Allsorts."

Taking precautions

After several unsuccessful years of searching for Mr Right, a woman decides to take out a personal ad. She ends up corresponding with a man who has lived his entire life in the Australian Outback; and, after a long-distance courtship, they decide to get married.

On their wedding night, she goes into the bathroom to prepare for the festivities. When she returns to the bedroom, she finds her new husband standing in the middle of the room, naked and all the furniture from the room piled in one corner.

"What's going on?" she asks.

"I've never been with a woman," he says. "But if it's anything like a kangaroo, I'm going to need all the room I can get!"

Decisions, decisions

A woman goes into a dentist's office and, after her examination, the dentist says to her, "I'm sorry to tell you this, but I'm going to have to drill that tooth."

Horrified, the woman replies, "Oh, no! I'd rather have a baby." The dentist replies, "Make up your mind; I have to adjust the chair."

How do you get 500 cows in a barn?
Put up a sign saying 'Bingo'.

Cheaper by the dozen

On the first day of a new university year, the freshers were given a speech about on-campus rules: "The female halls are out of bounds for all male students, and likewise the male halls to the female students," said the student union rep. "Anybody caught breaking this rule will be fined £20 the first time, £60 the second and £180 the third time. Any questions?"

At this point, a male student in the crowd raised his hand. "How much for a season ticket?"

Cut to the chase

A man walks into an antiques shop. After a while, he chooses a brass rat and brings it to the counter.

"That will be £10 for the brass rat and £1,000 for the story behind it," says the owner.

"Thanks, but I'll pay the £10 and pass on the story," replies the man.

So the man buys the brass rat and leaves the shop. As he walks down the street, he notices all sorts of rats following him. The further he walks, the more rats follow. He walks down to the pier and still more rats come out and follow him. So, he decides to walk out into the water and all the rats drown. Afterwards, he goes back to the shop.

"Ah-ha, you're back!" says the owner. "You've come back for the story, right?"

"Nope," says the man. "You got any brass lawyers?"

Look on the bright side

A group of OAPs were sitting around talking about their various ailments.

"My arms are so weak, I can hardly hold this cup of coffee," said one.

"Yes, I know," replied another.

"My cataracts are so bad I can't even see my coffee."

"I can't turn my head because of the arthritis in my neck,"

said a third, to which several nodded weakly in agreement.

"My blood pressure pills make me dizzy," another went on.

"I guess that's the price we pay for getting old," winced an old man.

Then there was a short moment of silence.

"Well, it's not that bad," said one woman cheerfully. "Thank God we can all still drive!"

Why did Frosty the Snowman get excited?
He heard the snowblower coming.

Monkey business

A man walks into a bar and sees a monkey in a cage. He asks the bartender, "What does the monkey do?"

The barman says, "I'll show you." He opens the cage door, hits the monkey on the head with a cricket bat and the monkey gives him oral sex.

The man is amazed and the bartender says, "You want to have a go?"

"Definitely," says the man,

That deserves some sort of prize

A married man was having an affair with his secretary. One day, their passions overcame them and they went to her house, where they made love. Afterwards, they fell asleep, only waking up at 8pm. As the man threw on his clothes, he told the woman to take his shoes outside and rub them through the grass and dirt. Mystified, she went ahead and did it. He then slipped into his shoes and drove home.

"Where have you been?" demanded his wife when he entered the house.

"Darling, I can't lie to you," he said. "I've been having an affair with my secretary and we've been having sex all afternoon. I fell asleep and didn't wake up until eight o'clock." The wife glanced down at his shoes and said, "You lying bastard! You've been playing golf."

The spirit is willing, but...

One afternoon, an elderly couple are relaxing in front of the TV. Suddenly, the woman is overcome with lust and says to her husband, "Let's go upstairs and make love." "Steady on," he replies. "I can't do both."

Honest mistake

A man was sprawled out across three entire seats in his local cinema. When the usher came by and noticed this, he whispered to the man, "Sorry, sir, but you're only allowed one seat."

The man groaned but didn't budge, and the usher became impatient.

"Sir," the usher repeated, "if you don't get up from there, I'm going to have to call the manager."

Again, the man just groaned, infuriating the usher, who then turned and marched briskly back up the aisle in search of his manager. In a few moments, both the usher and the manager returned and stood over the man. Together the two of them tried to move him, but with no success. Finally, they decided to call the police. Soon, a policeman arrived and surveyed the situation briefly.

"Alright, mate. What's your name?"

"Sam," the man moaned.

"Where you from, Sam?" the cop asked.

"The balcony."

Who's the king of the hankies?
The handkerchief.

Whoopee!

Jack and Bob are driving when they get caught in a blizzard. They pull into a nearby farmhouse and ask the attractive lady of the house if they can spend the night.

"I'm recently widowed," she explains, "and I'm afraid the neighbours will talk if I let you stay here."

"Not to worry," Jack says. "We'll be happy to sleep in the barn."

Nine months later, Jack gets a letter from the widow's attorney. After reading it, he quickly drives around to Bob's house.

"Bob, remember that good-looking widow at the farm we stayed at?"

"Yes, I remember her," says Bob.

"Did you happen to get up in the middle of the night, go up to the house and have sex with her?" asks Jack.

"Yes, I have to admit that I did," replies Bob.

"Did you happen to use my name instead of telling her your name?" asks Jack.

Embarrassed, Bob says, "Yeah, I'm afraid I did."

"Well, thanks a lot, pal," says Jack. "She just died and left me her farm!"

Why couldn't Rover bark?
Because he was a goldfish.

Narrow escape

A little guy goes into an elevator, looks up and sees a huge bloke next to him. The man sees the little fella staring at him, looks down and says, "Seven feet tall, 350 pounds, 20-inch penis, three-pound left testicle, three-pound right testicle, Turner Brown."

The small guy immediately faints and falls to the floor. The tall man kneels down and brings him to, slapping his face and shaking him. "What's wrong with you?" he asks.

In a very weak voice, the little guy says, "Excuse me, but what exactly did you say to me?"

The tall man answers, "I saw the curious look on your face and figured I'd just give you the answers to the questions everyone always asks me. I'm seven feet tall, 350 pounds, 20-inch penis, three-pound left testicle, three-pound right testicle, and my name is Turner Brown."

"Thank God for that," the small guy says. "I thought you said, 'Turn around.'"

Using your loaf

"We specialise in hygiene" said the sign at the bread shop and the customer was delighted when he saw the baker use tongs to pick up his rolls and put them in a bag.

"Untouched by human hands!" said the baker.

"Very good," said the customer as he immediately started to eat one of the rolls. "But tell me – what's that piece of string hanging out of your flies?"

"Hygiene," said the baker. "When I have a pee, I pull it out with the string."

"How do you put it back?" asked the customer.

"With the tongs, of course," replied the baker.

The old enemy

Before an England vs Scotland friendly, Wayne Rooney goes into the England changing room, only to find all his team-mates looking a bit glum.

"What's the matter, lads?" he asks.

"We're having trouble getting motivated for this game, Wayne," replies Becks. "We know we're playing for national pride but it's only Scotland. We can't really get all that excited."

Rooney looks at them and says, "Well, I reckon I can beat them single-handed. You lads have the afternoon off and watch from the pub."

So Rooney goes out to play Scotland all by himself and the rest of the squad nip off to the pub for a few pints. After a few jars they wonder how the game is going, so they get the landlord to put it on the TV. A big cheer goes up as the screen reads, "England 1 – Scotland 0 (Rooney, 10 minutes)". A few more pints of lager later, and Ashley Cole shouts out, "It must be full-time now, let's see how he got on."

They look up at the TV and see "England 1 (Rooney, 10 minutes) – Scotland 1 (Ferguson, 89 minutes)". The England team can't believe it – Rooney has managed a draw against the entire Scotland team. They all rush back to the stadium to congratulate him but find him in the dressing-room, sobbing, with his head in his hands. He refuses to look at them.

"I've let you down, lads," says Rooney.

"Don't be daft!" says Becks. "You got a draw against Scotland all by yourself, and they only scored in the 89th minute!"

"No, no. I have let you down," insists Rooney. "I got sent off in the 12th minute."

How many kids with Attention Deficit Hyperactivity Disorder does it take to change a light bulb?
Wanna ride bikes?

Now we're getting somewhere

A policeman pulls over a car for swerving and asks the driver to take a breathalyzer test.

"I can't do that," says the man. "I'm an asthmatic. The breathalyzer could bring on an attack."

So the policeman suggests a urine sample.

"Can't do it," says the man. "I'm a diabetic, so my urine always has strange stuff in it."

"Well," says the angry policeman, "why don't you just get out of the car and walk along this white line?"

"Sorry," says the man, "but I can't do that either."

"Why not?" asks the officer.

"Because I'm drunk."

Mutual satisfaction

A man drives his date up to Lovers' Lane and parks up.

"I have to be honest with you," the woman says as the man makes his move. "I'm a prostitute."

The man thinks about this for a bit and decides he's OK with it. He agrees to pay her £25 in advance and they get down to business.

After they finish, the man says, "Now, I should be honest, too. I'm a taxi driver and it's going to cost you £25 to get back into town."

First things first

A lawyer parks his brand-new Jaguar and, just as he steps out, a truck comes barrelling down the street and tears the driver's door clean off. The lawyer calls 999 and within five minutes the police are on the scene. But before he can start filling in his incident report, the copper is amazed to hear the lawyer screaming about how his new Jag is wrecked beyond repair. When the lawyer finally calms down, the cop shakes his head in disgust. "I can't believe how materialistic you lawyers are," he says. "You're so focused on your possessions that you don't notice anything else."

"How can you say such a thing?" the lawyer asks.

"For God's sake, man," the copper yells. "Your left arm is missing from the elbow down! It must have been torn off in the accident."

"Arrgh!" the lawyer cries. "Where's my Rolex?"

Don't you just hate it when that happens?

A cowboy walks into a saloon and says, "Who painted my horse's balls yellow?"

Suddenly, a huge, mean-looking cowboy stands up and says, "I did."

So the first guy looks up at him and says, "Great. The first coat's dry."

There, but for the grace of God...

A man placed some flowers on the grave of his mother and was starting back towards his car when his attention was diverted to another man kneeling at a grave. The man kept repeating, “Why did you have to die?”

The first man approached him and said, “I don’t wish to interfere with your private grief, but can I ask who you’re mourning for?”

The mourner took a moment to collect himself, then replied, “My wife’s first husband.”

Thanks for nothing

A woman’s husband has been slipping in and out of a coma for several months, yet she stays lovingly by his bedside every day. Finally, he comes to and motions for her to come near.

“You, my love,” he says, “have been with me through all the bad times. When I was fired, you were there for me. When the business failed, you were there. When I got shot, you were by my side. When we lost the house, you stood by me throughout. When my health started failing, you were still by my side. You know what?”

“What, dear?” she asks, gently.

“I think you bring me bad luck.”

That's why I don't believe in you

An atheist explorer in the deepest Amazon suddenly finds himself surrounded by a group of bloodthirsty natives. Upon surveying the situation, he says quietly to himself, "Oh, God. I'm screwed this time!"

There is a ray of light from Heaven and a voice booms out, "No, you are not screwed. All you have to do is pick up that stone at your feet and bash in the head of the chief standing in front of you."

So the explorer picks up the stone and proceeds to bash the chief until he's unconscious.

As he stands above the body, breathing heavily and surrounded by hundreds of natives with looks of shock and anger on their faces, God's voice booms out again and says, "OK... now you're screwed."

Quick thinking

One fine spring day, a farmer walks through his orchard to a nearby pond, carrying a bucket of fruit. Once there, he spies two sexy young women skinny-dipping. Spotting him, they duck down below the water so that only their heads are visible.

"We're not coming out until you leave!" shouts one of the girls.

Thinking on his feet, the farmer replies: "Oh, I'm not here to see you two – just here to feed the piranhas!"

A lesson for life

Once upon a time, there lived an orphaned bunny and an orphaned snake who were both blind from birth. One day, the two met and decided to help one another out.

"Maybe I could slither all over you, and work out what you are," hissed the snake. "Oh, that would be wonderful," replied the bunny.

So the snake slithered all over the bunny, and said, "Well, you're covered with soft fur, your nose twitches, and you have a soft, cottony tail. I'd say that you must be a bunny rabbit."

The bunny then suggested to the snake, "Maybe I could feel you all over with my paw, and help you find out what you are." So the bunny felt the snake all over, and said, "Well, you're slippery, you have no backbone and no balls. I'd say you must be either a team leader, supervisor or management."

Bird brain

A man follows a woman with a parrot out of a cinema, stops her and says, "I'm sorry to bother you, but I couldn't help noticing that your bird seemed to understand the film. He cried at the right parts, and he laughed at the jokes. Don't you find that unusual?"

"I do indeed," she replies. "He hated the book."

Wisdom of age

Three old men are at the hospital for a memory test.

"What's three times three?" the doctor asks the first old man.

"Two hundred and seventy-four," he replies.

"What's three times three?" the doctor asks the second old man.

"Tuesday," he replies.

The doctor quickly realises he's in for a very long morning.

He turns to the third old man and asks, "OK, your turn. What's three times three?"

"Nine," he replies.

"Yes!" exclaims the doctor. "How did you get that?"

"Easy. I just subtracted 274 from Tuesday."

What's the difference between worry and panic?
About 28 days.

Rules are rules

A brain and two turds go into a pub. The barman says to the brain, "I'm not serving you. Get out!" The brain asks why, and so the barman replies, "Because you're out of your head and your two mates are steaming!"

If that don't beat all...

Three cowboys are sitting in the bunkhouse. "That smart-arse Tex," says the first. "He's going to start bragging about that new foreign car he bought as soon as he comes in."

"Not Tex," says the second. "He's just a good ol' boy. When he walks in, I'm sure all he'll say is, 'Hello'."

"I know Tex better than any of you," says the third. "He's so smart, he'll figure out a way to do both. Here he comes now."

Tex then swings open the bunkhouse door and shouts, "Audi, partners!"

Child prodigy

Little Johnny returned home from school, informing his father that he'd received an F in maths and a detention.

"What happened?" asked his dad.

"Well," little Johnny said, "the teacher asked, 'How much is two times three?' and I said 'Six'."

"But that's right!" said his father.

"Then," said Johnny, "she asked, 'How much is three times two?'"

"That's crap. What's the difference?" asked his father.

"That's what I said!"

What will Postman Pat be called when he retires?
Pat.

I wink, therefore I am

A man with a winking problem applies for a position as a travelling sales rep and goes in for the interview.

"You're more than qualified," says the interviewer, "but we can't have our sales reps constantly winking at customers. We can't hire you."

"But wait," says the man. "If I take two aspirin, I stop winking."

"Show me," replies the interviewer.

The man then reaches into his pocket and pulls out a pile of condoms in all different shapes, sizes and colours before finally finding a packet of aspirin. He takes the pill and immediately stops winking.

"That's great," says the interviewer, "but we can't have our reps womanising all the time."

"I'm happily married," gasps the man.

"And the condoms?" asks the interviewer.

"Oh," sighs the man. "Well, have you ever tried walking into a chemist, winking and asking for aspirin?"

Marital relations

Mr Johnson and his secretary are on a first-class flight. As they're nodding off for the night, the secretary, who has long had a crush on her boss, says in her most seductive voice, "I'm a little cold. Can I get under your blanket?"

Reading her signals clearly, the boss says, "How would you like to be Mrs Johnson for a while?"

"I'd love it!" the secretary replies, jumping at the chance.

"Great," Mr Johnson says, "then get your own damn blanket."

Divine protection

Reggie Kray dies and goes to Heaven. At the Pearly Gates, Saint Peter asks his name.

"Kray. Reginald," he replies.

Saint Peter looks him up on the computer and it comes up on his database with a list of crimes as long as his arm.

Worried, Saint Peter goes to check with God before he can let him in.

"This is no good," says God. "Send him downstairs to Hell."

Saint Peter goes back out to the gates and says, "I'm sorry, Mr Kray, but we can't let you in."

To which Reggie replies, "I don't want to come in. I want £2,000 a week or I'm shutting you down."

Suspicious minds

A worried man calls up his best mate in a panic. "I really need your advice, pal. I'm desperate and I don't know what to do."

His friend replies, "Sure, I'll try and help. What's wrong?"

The worried man explains: "For some time now, I've suspected that my wife may be cheating on me. You know the sort of thing; the phone rings, I answer, someone hangs up."

"That's terrible, mate," says his friend.

"That's not all," continues the worried man. "The other day, I picked up her mobile, just to see what time it was, and she went mental, screaming at me that I should never touch her phone again, and that I was checking up on her. So far I haven't confronted her about it. I sort of think, deep down, I don't really want to know the truth. But then, last night, she went out again and I decided to check up on her. I hid behind my car, which I knew would give me a good view of the whole street. That way, I could see which car she got out of on her return. Anyway, it was while I was crouched behind my car that I noticed some rust around the rear wheel arch. So, do you think I should take it into a body repair shop, or just buy some of that stuff from Halfords and try to sort it out myself?"

What do you call cheese that's not yours?
Nachocheese.

Youth versus age

A young naval student is asked by an old sea captain: "What would you do if a sudden storm sprang up on the starboard?"

"Throw out an anchor, sir," the student replies, promptly.

"And what would you do if a storm sprang up aft?"

"Throw out another anchor, sir," comes back the student.

"And if another terrific storm sprang up forward, what would you do?" says the captain.

"Throw out another anchor," replies the student.

"Hold on," says the captain. "Where are you getting all your anchors from?"

"Same place you're getting your storms, sir."

How are politicians like nappies?
You have to change them frequently, and for the same reason.

Raise your glasses

A man walks into a pub, sits down, orders three pints of lager, drinks them and then leaves. This continues daily for several weeks.

Curious, the pub landlord approaches him one day. "Why do you always order three pints of lager?" he asks.

"Well," says the man, "my two brothers and I always used to have a pint each and since they've both passed on, I've continued to order the three beers in their honour."

The landlord is taken aback by such nobility and welcomes the man whenever he then visits the pub. But two weeks later, the man strolls in and orders not his usual three pints, but only two. Surprised, the landlord asks what the problem is.

"Oh, no problem at all," smiles the man. "I've just decided to stop drinking."

Your call

A husband and wife are watching *Who Wants To Be A Millionaire?* It gets the husband thinking and he looks over at his wife, winks and says, "Honey, let's go upstairs."

"No," sighs his wife.

The husband looks at her and says, "Is that your final answer?"

"Yes," she replies.

"In that case," smiles hubby, "can I phone a friend?"

What do the Inland Revenue, an ostrich and a pelican all have in common?
They can all stick their bills up their arses.

Chop, chop!

A man sticks his head into a hairdresser's and asks, "How long is the wait?"

"About two hours," the barber says, and the man leaves.

A few days later, the same man pokes his head in and again asks, "How long is the wait?"

"About two hours," the barber replies. The guy leaves again.

A week later, the man pops in and asks the same question.

The barber replies, "About an hour."

Once again, the man leaves, but this time the barber sends his friend to follow the man. His mate returns later, looking sheepish.

"So where does he go after leaving my shop?" the barber asks.

"Your house," his mate replies.

Wonders of modern technology

A man walks into a pub, orders a beer and begins punching his hand with his finger as if he was dialling a phone.

"What are you doing, mate?" asks the very curious landlord.

"I've had a phone installed in my hand because I was tired of carrying one around," the man answers. "Try it!"

The man dials a number and puts his hand up to the landlord's ear. The owner of the pub across the street picks up and the landlord can't believe it.

"Amazing, eh?" says the man. "Now, where's the gents?"

The landlord tells him, but when the man doesn't come back for over an hour, the landlord goes looking for him. He finds him in the gents, spread-eagled against the wall with his trousers around his ankles and a roll of toilet paper coming out of his underpants.

"My God!" the landlord yells. "Were you mugged?"

The man turns to him and says, "No, I'm fine. Just waiting for a fax."

What's the definition of a happy transvestite?
A guy who likes to eat, drink and be Mary.

Fashion victim

David Beckham is walking through the jungle with Posh when he suddenly turns to her and says, “Look at that flash bastard with the all-in-one Lacoste sleeping bag.”

Hear about the flasher who was thinking of retiring?
He’s sticking it out for a while longer.

Mysterious ways

A drunken priest is pulled over for speeding. Smelling alcohol on the father’s breath and noticing a wine bottle on the passenger seat, the copper asks, “Sir, have you been drinking?”

The minister replies, “Just water.”

“Then tell me,” the policeman enquires. “How is it that I can smell wine?”

The minister looks down at the bottle and exclaims, “Good Lord, He’s done it again!”

Game of skill

The owner of a petrol station tries to boost sales by posting a sign that says, "Free sex with every fill-up."

Before long, two rednecks pull in. The driver gets out, fills his tank and then enquires about the offer.

"Pick a number between one and ten," says the owner. "If you guess correctly, you win free sex!"

The customer thinks for a bit, then finally guesses eight.

"No, but you were really close," smiles the owner. "The actual number was seven. Better luck next time, eh?"

As the two men pull away, the driver says to his mate, "You know what, I reckon that game was rigged. I bet you he doesn't really give away free sex at all."

"Oh no, it ain't rigged," replies his mate. "My wife won three times last week..."

Keeping up appearances

A man weds his virgin bride and on the big night, strips off and jumps into bed for a grope. Taken aback, his new wife lays down the law. "I expect you to be as well-mannered in bed as you are at the dinner table, my love!"

"Oh right," says the man, backing off a bit. "Well, then, will you please pass the sex?"

Going bananas

A gorilla walks into a bar and orders a pint of lager. The barman charges him five quid and, after looking at him for a while, says, "Do you know, you're the first gorilla we've had in here for ages?"

"I'm not bloody surprised," replies the gorilla, "at a fiver a pint."

Have you heard about the new super-sensitive condom?
It hangs around after the man leaves and gives the woman a hug.

Signs of stress

A psychology tutor is giving her class an oral test on mental health. Singling out a student, she grills him on manic depression: "How would you diagnose a patient who walks back and forth screaming at the top of his lungs one minute, then sits in a chair weeping uncontrollably the next?"

The young man thinks for a moment, then offers his answer: "Premiership manager?"

If you must

A man is pleasuring a lady. "Would you like to try the social security position?" he asks her.

"What on earth is that?" she replies.

"Well," explains the man, "when my balls are touching your arse, you're getting full benefit!"

Oh, God

A burglar breaks into a house and creeps into a room with no lights on. He walks into the room and hears a voice which says, "Jesus is watching you."

The thief turns around and, in a dark corner of the room, he sees a parrot. As he creeps over to shut the bird up, the parrot shrieks again, "Jesus is watching you."

The annoyed burglar looks at the parrot and asks, "What's your name?" The parrot replies, "Clarence."

The burglar laughs and, as he's about to throttle the bird, says, "That's a stupid name for a parrot. What idiot called you that?"

The parrot replies, "The same idiot who decided to call the rottweiler Jesus."

What do you call an insect that flies around a lampshade at 180mph?
Stirling Moth.

Personal services

A man is sitting at a bar enjoying a drink when an exceptionally gorgeous young woman walks in. The man can't take his eyes off her. Noticing his overly attentive stare, she walks directly over to him and, before he can even apologise for gawping, she makes him an offer: "I'll do absolutely anything you want me to, no matter how kinky it is, for £100. However, there is one condition..."

Naturally, the man asks what the condition is. "Well," says the woman, "you have to tell me what you want me to do in three words."

The man considers the proposition for a moment, takes out his wallet and slowly counts out five £20 notes. He presses each note into the young woman's hand, looks excitedly into her eyes and finally says: "Paint my house."

What's black and white and red all over?
A cow that's just been murdered.

A short life, but a merry one

A man bursts into a busy pub, points to his left and shouts, "All the arseholes over that side!"

He then points to his right and shouts, "All the dickheads get over that side!"

Suddenly, the hardest guy in the pub stands up and says, "Who are you calling a dickhead?"

The man points to his left and shouts, "Over there, arsehole!"

It brings it all back

A local reporter goes to an old people's home to interview an ageing but legendary explorer. After hearing many incredible tales, he asks the old man to tell him about the most frightening experience he ever had on his travels.

"Once, I was hunting tigers in the jungles of India. I was on a narrow path and my native guide was behind me, carrying my rifle. Just then, the largest tiger I've ever seen leapt out in front of us. I turned around for my weapon only to find that the native had fled. The tiger pounced at me with a mighty 'Roarrrr!' I'm sorry to say I soiled myself."

The reporter says, "Sir, don't be embarrassed. Under those circumstances anyone would have done the same."

"No, not then," the old man replies. "Just now, when I went 'Roarrrr!'"

What do you call a bear without a paw?
A bastard.

Kill yourself now

A man has huge feet. Wherever he goes, people take the mick. Sitting on the beach wall with his plates dangling in the water, a vicar strolls past and can see the man is upset, so he walks over and asks, "What's the matter?"

"I'm so depressed," replies the man. "Everywhere I go, people ridicule me for the size of my feet."

The vicar comes up with a plan and tells the man, "Dye your hair a brilliant green and, that way, people will look at your hair and not your feet!"

The man thanks the vicar for the advice, goes to the nearest hair salon and has his hair dyed. He walks out feeling fantastic – better than he's felt in a long time. He bounds down the road and a passer-by shouts out, "Hey, you with the green hair!"

He turns around and shouts confidently back, "Yeah?"

"Ha, ha," laughs the passer-by. "You've got bloody massive feet, mate!"

There are two grains of sand in the desert.
One turns to the other and says, "Busy here, isn't it?"

Best of friends

Spotting a monkey at the side of the road, a truck driver pulls over, opens the passenger door and asks, "Do you need a lift?"

The monkey hops in but, as they drive off, a policeman pulls them over.

"I want you to take that monkey to the zoo," the officer barks.

"Yeah, I suppose that would be the best thing to do with him," the truck driver agrees.

The next day, the policeman sees the monkey sitting in the same truck. So, he pulls the trucker over again and says, "I thought I told you to take that monkey to the zoo!"

The trucker replies, "Oh, I did, officer, and we had a great time. Today we're going fishing."

What's black and white and eats like a horse?
A zebra.

Crime against humanity

An accordionist is driving home from a late-night gig. Feeling tired, he pulls into a service station for some coffee. While waiting to pay, he remembers that he locked his car doors but left the accordion in plain view on the back seat of his car! He rushes out only to realise that he is too late. The back window of his car has been smashed and somebody's already thrown in two more accordions.

Well, when you put it like that...

A motorist screeches to a halt on a garage forecourt, looking for the man who sold him his car.

"Oi!" he shouts at a salesman. "I want a bloody word with you."

"What's the matter, sir?" says the salesman. "Everything OK with your car?"

"No, everything is not OK with my car. I bought this heap on the understanding that it was going to give me good performance and it'll only get to 110 uphill. It's ridiculous."

Taken aback, the salesman says, "Well, excuse me, sir, but I must point out that 110 uphill is very impressive for a car in this class."

"Impressive?" the man yells. "Not when I live at 136 it's not!"

What do you call 12 naked men sitting on each others' shoulders?
A scrotum pole.

So long, suckers!

A tour bus driver is driving a bus full of OAPs on holiday when a little old lady taps him on his shoulder. She offers him a handful of almonds, which he gratefully munches down.

After about 15 minutes, she taps him on his shoulder again and she hands him another handful of almonds. She repeats this gesture about eight times. At the ninth time, he asks the little old lady why they don't eat the almonds themselves? She explains that because of their false teeth, they can't chew them.

"Why do you buy them then?" the puzzled driver asks.

The old lady answers, "We just love the chocolate around them."

Why did the horse win the Nobel Prize?
Because he was out standing in his field.

Mustn't grumble

Morris and his wife, Esther, went to the funfair every year. And every year, Morris would say, "Esther, I'd like to ride in that helicopter."

Esther always replied, "Yes, it looks fun, Morris, but that helicopter ride is £50 – and £50 is £50."

One year later, Esther and Morris went to the fair again. Morris said, "Esther, I'm 85 years old. If I don't ride that helicopter now, I might never get another chance."

Esther replied, "That's all very well, Morris, but that helicopter ride is £50 – and £50 is £50."

The pilot overheard the couple. He said, "Folks, I'll make you a deal. I'll take both of you for a ride. If you can stay quiet for the entire ride and not say a word, I won't charge you. But if you say one word, it's £50."

Morris and Esther agreed and up they went. The pilot did all kinds of fancy manoeuvres, but not a word was heard. He did his daredevil tricks over and over again, but still not a word. When they landed, the pilot turned to Morris and said, "Blimey! I did everything I could to get you to yell out, but you didn't. I'm impressed!"

Morris replied, "Well, I was going to say something when Esther fell out halfway through, but £50 is £50."

Beyond the pale

A retiring golf club president is making his final speech at his club's annual awards ceremony. "From 18-handicappers to pros, I've treated everyone equally," the emotional president begins. "We all live for this game. We're like a big family and after all these years together I only fell by the wayside once. While my darling wife sits beside me, I want to apologise to her and you, my beloved friends. In a mere moment of weakness, I betrayed her. It meant nothing – a one-night stand, that's all."

After this shocking revelation, the president sits down, ashamed. His wife rises, smiling as ever. "I, too, have a confession, darling," she says. "Before I met you, I was a man!"

There are gasps around the room as the startled president staggers back to his feet. "You cheating bastard!" he exclaims. "All these years you played off the front tees."

What should you do if you're attacked by a gang of clowns?
Go for the juggler.

All right, you asked for it!

A primary school teacher was trying to get her class to stop speaking in 'baby talk' and insisting on 'big people' words only.

She asked Chris what he had done over the weekend.

"I visited my nana, Miss," said Chris.

"No, you went to visit your grandmother. We're using 'big people' words here, Chris!"

She then asked Rupert what he had done.

"I took a ride on a choo-choo, Miss," replied Rupert.

The teacher said, "No, Rupert, you took a ride on a train. You must remember to use 'big people' words."

She then asked little Alex what he had done.

"I read a book, Miss," he replied.

"That's wonderful!" the teacher said. "What book did you read?"

Alex thought for a second, before saying, "Winnie the Shit, Miss."

How is sex like air?
It's not a big deal unless you're not getting any.

The truth will out

A mum is driving her little girl to a friend's house to play.

"Mummy," the little girl asks. "How old are you?"

"You aren't supposed to ask a lady her age," the mother warns. "It's personal and it is not polite."

"OK," the little girl says. "Why did you and Daddy get a divorce?"

"That's enough questions. Honestly!" exclaims the exasperated mother, before walking away as the two friends begin to play.

"My mum wouldn't tell me anything," the little girl says to her friend.

"Well," said the friend. "All you need to do is look at her birth certificate. It has everything on it."

Later that night, the little girl says to her mother, "I know how old you are. You're 32."

The mother is surprised and asks, "How did you find that out?"

"And," the little girl says, triumphantly, "I know why you and Daddy got a divorce."

"Oh, really?" the mother asks, somewhat surprised. "And why's that?"

"Because you only got an F in sex."

That sinking feeling

Three men are walking through the jungle when a native tribe ambushes them. The leader of the tribe offers each man one last request before being killed for trespassing. The first man asks for a big feast, so the tribe give him their best food and when he's full, they chop off his head.

"We shall make him into a canoe!" the leader exclaims.

The next man pleads to have sex one last time, so the tribe gets their sexiest woman and he has the best sex of his life. Then the tribe chop off his head and again the leader says, "We shall make him into a canoe!"

The last man thinks for a second, then requests a fork. The tribe look confused, but give him a fork. Then the man starts to stab himself all over and shouts, "You're not making a bloody canoe out of me!"

Where do you get virgin wool from?
Ugly sheep.

What does a redneck always say just before he dies?
"Hey! Watch this."

Ding-dong!

Upon hearing that her elderly grandfather had just passed away, Kate went to her grandparents' house to visit her 95-year-old grandmother.

When she asked how her grandfather had died, her grandmother replied, "He had a heart attack while we were making love on Sunday morning."

Horrified, the woman told her grandmother that two people nearly 100 years old having sex would surely be asking for trouble.

"Oh no, my dear," replied Granny. "Many years ago, we figured out that the best time to do it was when the church bells started to ring. It was just the right rhythm – nice and slow and even. Nothing too strenuous for us."

She paused to wipe away a tear, and continued, "He'd still be alive if the ice-cream van hadn't come along."

The birds and the bees

Two boys get their grades from their female sex education teacher. One gets a D and the other an F.

"We should get her for this," says the first boy.

"Yeah," the second agrees. "I'm going to kick her right in the nuts."

How do you keep a kid from wetting the bed?
Give him an electric blanket.

The inevitable duck/pub joke

A duck walks into a bar and orders a pint of beer.

Amazed, the bartender says, "Hey, you can talk!"

"Sure, pal," says the duck. "Now can I get that drink?"

Shaking his head, the barman serves the duck a pint and asks him what he's doing in the area.

"I work on the building site across the street," says the duck.

"You should join the circus," says the barman. "You could make a mint."

"The circus?" the duck replies. "What the hell would the circus want with a bricklayer?"

Now that's magic

A man finds a magic lamp, rubs it and a genie pops out: "I grant you three wishes, but for every wish you make, your mother-in-law gets double whatever it is you request!"

The man agrees and the genie asks for his first wish.

"I want to have £100million!" says the man. The genie duly grants his wish, but warns that his mother-in-law now has £200million.

"For my second wish," says the man, "I want to be famous!"

No problem for the genie – the man is famous. But his mother-in-law is twice as famous.

Several quiet, thoughtful minutes pass before the man suggests his final wish: "Genie – beat me half to death!"

Spit and polish

Pinocchio moaned to Gepetto that when he made love to his girlfriend she complained about splinters.

"Try some sandpaper, Pinocchio," advised Gepetto.

A month later Gepetto asked, "How's your love life, then? Is your girlfriend still complaining of splinters?"

"Who needs a girlfriend?" replied Pinocchio.

Never too old

Bert, 92, and Agnes, 89, are about to get married. They go for a stroll to discuss the wedding, and on the way they pass a chemist. Bert suggests they go in.

Bert first asks the pharmacist, "Do you sell heart medication?"

Pharmacist: "Of course."

Bert: "How about medicine for circulation?"

Pharmacist: "All kinds."

Bert: "How about Viagra?"

Pharmacist: "Of course."

Bert: "Do you sell wheelchairs and walkers?"

Pharmacist: "We do – all speeds and sizes."

Bert: "That's brilliant! We'd like to use this shop for our wedding list, please."

"Knock, knock."
"Who's there?"
"Control freak. Now this is where you say, 'Control freak who?'"

What did Cinderella say when she left Boots?
"Some day my prints will come."

Sleeping partner

A man gets taken on as a lorry driver at a new company but as he's about to sign his contract in the boss's office, he says, "I've got one demand. Since you employed me, you've got to hire my mate, Dave, too."

"Who's Dave?" says the boss, surprised at the demand.

"Dave's my driving partner. We're a team. He drives when I sleep, and I drive when he sleeps," the new employee says.

"OK," says the boss. "Answer this question satisfactorily and I'll hire your mate too. You're going down a hill, your brakes fail, and ahead of you is a bridge with an 18-wheeler jack-knifed across it. What would you do?"

"I'd wake Dave up," he replies.

"How the hell's that going to help?" says the boss.

"We've been working together 25 years," explains the new guy, "and he's never seen a wreck like the one we're about to have!"

Cabin pressure

A man is on a low-budget flight to Amsterdam, waiting for take-off. Another bloke comes up and says, "Excuse me, but you're in my seat."

"Don't think so. First come, first served with this airline, mate," responds the man, remaining seated.

"Look here," the newcomer insists, "I fly to Amsterdam every day and I sit in that seat every day! Now, do I have to go and get a flight attendant?"

"Get whoever you want," shrugs the seated man.

Annoyed, the other man disappears for a short while and returns with a flight attendant. "I'm sorry, sir, but I'm going to have to ask you to choose another seat," she says.

The man stands up, picks up his bag in a huff and says, "Fine. I didn't want to fly the plane anyway!"

What do you call a randy dwarf?
A low blow.

Why doesn't Mexico have an Olympic team?
Because everybody who can run, jump or swim is already in the US.

Healing touch

Two women were playing golf. One teed off and watched in horror as her ball sailed towards a foursome of men playing the next hole. The ball hit one of the men, and he immediately clasped his groin, fell to the ground and rolled around in agony. The woman rushed down to the man and immediately began to apologise.

"Please let me help. I'm a physical therapist and I know I could relieve your pain if you'd allow me," she told him.

"Oh, no. I'll be all right. I'll be fine in a few minutes," the man replied, still in pain.

But she persisted, and he finally allowed her to help. She gently took his hands away, loosened his trousers and put her hands inside. She began to massage him. She then asked, "How does that feel?"

He replied, "It feels great, but my thumb still hurts like hell."

What are the three main food groups?
Fast, frozen and instant.

Shellshocked

A man walks into a pub holding a turtle. The turtle has two bandaged legs, a black eye and his shell is held together with duct tape. The landlord asks, "What's wrong with your turtle?" "Nothing," the man responds. "This turtle's very fast. Have your dog stand at the end of the bar. Then go and stand at the other end of the room and call him. Before that mutt reaches you, my turtle will be there." So the landlord, wanting to see this, sets his dog at one side of the room. Then he goes to the other side and calls him. Suddenly, the guy picks up his bandaged turtle and throws it across the room, narrowly missing the landlord and smashing it into the wall. "Told you!"

Cheep at the price

A guy walks into a pet shop wanting to buy a parrot. The owner shows him a parrot that has beautiful feathers, speaks English and costs £1,000. He shows him another one with even more beautiful feathers that speaks English, French and Italian, and it can use a word processor. It costs £3,000. Then the guy sees a parrot in a cage in a corner of the shop. It's rather small and has only grey feathers.

"How much for this one?"

"£5,000," replies the owner.

"£5,000!" the guy exclaims. "Does it speak foreign languages?"

"No."

"Does it have any skills?"

"Not that I know of," the owner says. "It just sits there all day."

"Then why is it £5,000?"

"The other two call it Boss."

My compliments to the chef

A resident in a posh hotel breakfast room calls over the head waiter one morning.

"Good morning, sir," says the waiter. "What would you like for breakfast today?"

"I'd like two boiled eggs, one of them so undercooked it's runny and the other so overcooked it's tough and hard to eat. Also, grilled bacon that has been left out so it gets a bit on the cold side; burnt toast that crumbles away as soon as you touch it with a knife; butter straight from the deep freeze so that it's impossible to spread and a pot of very weak coffee, lukewarm."

"That's a complicated order, sir," said the bewildered waiter. "It might be quite difficult."

The guest replied, "Oh? I don't understand why. That's exactly what I got yesterday."

That's what – ugh – you think

An old man goes to the doctor and says, "Doctor, I have this problem with farting, but it really doesn't bother me too much. They never smell and are always silent. As a matter of fact, I've farted at least 20 times since I've been here in your office. You didn't know I was passing gas, you see, because, as I say, they're odourless and noiseless."

The doctor says, "I see. Take these pills and come back to see me next week."

The next week the man goes back. "Doctor," he says, "I don't know what the heck you gave me, but now when I fart they're still silent but they stink terribly."

"Good," the doctor said. "Now that we've cleared up your sinuses, let's get to work on your hearing."

What's the difference between dogs and foxes? About four pints.

Sober judgement

A man goes into a lawyer's office and says, "I heard people have sued tobacco companies for giving them lung cancer."

The lawyer says, "Yes, that's perfectly true."

The man says, "Well, I'm interested in sueing someone, too."

The lawyer says, "OK. Who are you talking about?"

The man replies, "I'd like to sue all the breweries for the ugly women I've slept with."

Another for the feminists

Scientists have recently suggested that men should take a look at their beer consumption, considering the results of a recent analysis that revealed the presence of female hormones in beer. The theory is that drinking beer makes men turn into women. To test the finding, 100 men were fed six pints of lager each. It was then observed that 100 per cent of the men gained weight, talked excessively without making sense, became overly emotional, couldn't drive, failed to think rationally, argued over nothing and refused to apologise when wrong. No further testing is planned.

Don't speak too soon

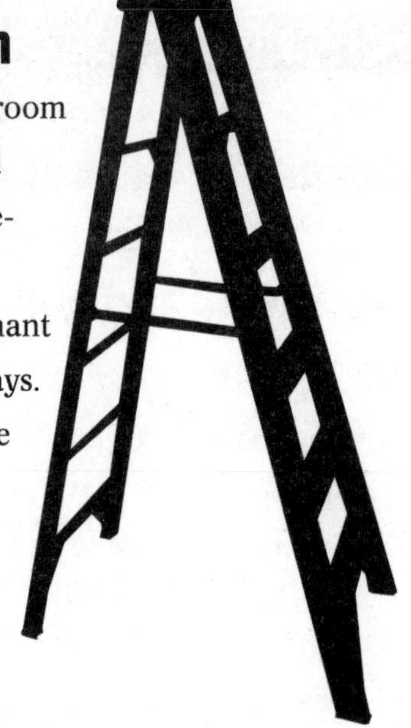

A fireman climbs up to the bedroom window of a burning house and finds a gorgeous blonde in a see-through nightie.

"Aha! You're the second pregnant girl I've rescued this year," he says.

"I'm not pregnant!" the blonde exclaims.

"You're not rescued yet, either."

His secret shame

Little David was in his primary class when the teacher asked the children what their fathers did for a living. All the typical answers came up: fireman; policeman; salesman. David was being uncharacteristically quiet, so the teacher asked him about his father. "My father's an exotic dancer in a gay cabaret and he takes off all his clothes in front of other men," he replied.

The teacher, obviously shaken by this statement, took little David aside to ask him, "Is that really true about your father?"

"No," said David. "He plays for Glasgow Rangers, but I was too embarrassed to say that in front of the other kids."

What do you do with a three-legged dog?
Take it for a drag.

Insert cockatoo pun here

A honeymooning couple buy a talking parrot and take it to their room, but the groom becomes annoyed when it keeps a running commentary on his lovemaking. Finally, he throws a towel over the cage and threatens to give the bird to the zoo if it doesn't keep quiet.

Early the next morning, the couple have trouble closing a suitcase.

"You get on top and I'll try," the groom instructs. But that doesn't work. The new bride figures they need more weight on top of the suitcase to shut it.

"You try getting on top," she says.

Still no success. Finally, the groom says, "Look, let's both get on top."

At this point the parrot uses his beak to pull the towel off and says, "Zoo or no zoo, I have to see this!"

Smart move

Amazingly, a 65-year-old woman has a baby. All her relatives come to visit and meet the newest member of their family. They all ask if they can see the baby, but the mother keeps saying, “Not yet.”

Finally, a cousin asks, “When can we see the baby?”

“When it cries,” says the elderly mother.

“But why do we have to wait until the baby cries?” the cousin asks, impatiently.

“Because I’ve forgotten where I’ve put it.”

His feminine side

Dave is at work when he notices that his colleague, Joe, is wearing an earring. Dave has always known Joe to be quite a conservative fella and is curious about his sudden change.

“Hey,” he yells out. “I didn’t know you were into earrings.”

“Don’t make such a big deal out of it,” says Joe.

“No, really,” probes Dave. “How long have you been wearing one?”

“Pretty much ever since my wife found it in our bed.”

I didn't want this job anyway

A young businessman is leaving the office late one night when he finds his boss standing over the shredder with a piece of paper in his hand.

"This is a very sensitive official document," says the boss. "My secretary's gone for the night. Can you make this thing work?"

"Sure," says the keen underling as he takes the paper, puts it in the shredder and hits the start button.

"Great," says his boss. "I just need the one copy, thanks."

Ask an expert

A scientific study has found that the kind of male face a woman finds attractive can differ depending on where she is in her menstrual cycle. For instance, if she is ovulating, she is attracted to men with rugged and masculine features. If she is menstruating, she is likely to prefer a man doused in petrol and set on fire, with scissors shoved deep into his temple. Further studies are expected.

What do you get when you mix a laxative with holy water?
A religious movement.

Unless it was a putter, obviously

A golf club walks into a local bar and asks the barman for a pint of beer.

"Sorry, mate, but I'm not supposed to serve you," says the barman.

"Why not?" says the golf club.

"You'll be driving later," replies the bartender.

Disaster management

Bill Gates dies and goes to Heaven. At the door, Saint Peter fits him with a £5,000 suit for everything he's achieved on earth. Later, as Bill's walking around Heaven, he sees a man with a much more expensive-looking suit than his. The computer genius is extremely angry with this so he goes to Saint Peter and says, "This man has a more expensive suit than me. Who is he?"

Saint Peter says, "Ah, that's the captain of the Titanic."

Bill is furious at this and argues, "But I created the Windows operating system and I get less than him?"

Saint Peter replies, "The Titanic only crashed once!"

The little woman

A man is giving a colleague a lift to work and asks him if he talks to his wife after sex.

"Absolutely," he says. "If I can find a phone."

What goes "Oooooooooo"?
A cow with no lips.

Land of the brave, home of the free

A redneck is walking down the road and sees his cousin coming toward him with a sack.

"What you got there?" he asks.

"Some chickens," replies his equally slack-jawed cousin.

"If I can guess how many you got, can I have one?"

"Shoot. If you guess right, I'll give you both of 'em."

"OK... five."

What is a man's view of safe sex?
A padded headboard.

You're a lifesaver

A man goes on holiday to the Caribbean, quickly falls asleep on the sand and ends up with a terrible sunburn. Wincing in pain as even a slight wind touches his scorched skin, the man hobbles off to the local doctor for help. The doctor takes one look at the man's legs and says, "I don't have anything to treat sunburn that bad. Try taking these Viagra pills."

"I've got sunburn!" cries the man. "What the hell's Viagra going to do?"

"Well, nothing for the sunburn," the doctor replies. "But it will help keep the sheets off your legs tonight."

I'm afraid our time is up...

A woman went to her psychiatrist because she was having problems with her sex life. The psychiatrist asked her many questions. Finally, he asked, "Do you ever watch your husband's face while you're having sex?"

"Well, yes, I actually did once," replied the woman.

"And tell me, how did your husband look?" asked the psychiatrist.

"Angry. Fuming, actually," replied the woman.

At this point, the psychiatrist felt that he was getting somewhere and said, "Well, that's interesting. How did it occur that you saw his face that time?"

"He was looking at me through the window!"

Snap diagnosis

While making his rounds, a doctor points out an X-ray to a group of medical students.

"As you can see," he begins, "the patient has a limp because his left fibula and tibia are radically arched."

The doctor turns to one of the students and asks, "What would you do in a case like this?"

"Well," ponders the student, "I suppose I'd limp, too."

What makes men chase women they have no intention of marrying?
The same urge that makes dogs chase cars they have no intention of driving.

Works like a charm

A man approaches a beautiful woman in a supermarket and asks, "You know, I've lost my wife here in the supermarket. Can you talk to me for a couple of minutes?"

"Why?" she asks.

"Because every time I talk to a beautiful woman, my wife appears out of nowhere."

Is this it?

Not long after their wedding, Scott and Lisa awake early one morning. They are up for quite a while before they meet in the kitchen. Marriage has been agreeing with Scott, and he greets his new wife with glee.

"Sweetheart," he says, "if you'll just make the toast and pour the juice, breakfast will be ready."

"Great! What are we having?" asks Lisa.

"Toast and juice," replies Scott.

Why do bagpipers walk when they play?
To get away from the sound.

Too close

A guy goes into a girl's house and she shows him into the living room. She excuses herself to go to the kitchen to make some drinks. As he's standing there alone, he notices a vase on the mantelpiece.

He picks it up and as he's looking at it, she walks back in. He says, "What's this?"

"Oh, my father's ashes are in there," she replies.

Turning red, he apologizes.

She continues, "Yeah, he's too lazy to go to get an ashtray."

He's got you there

A mechanic was removing the cylinder head from the engine of a Jaguar when he spotted a well-known heart surgeon in his garage, who was waiting for the service manager to look at his car.

The mechanic shouted across the garage, "Hey, Doc. Could I ask you a question?"

The surgeon, a bit surprised, walked over to the mechanic.

The mechanic straightened up, wiped his hands on a rag and asked, "So, Doc, take a look at this engine. I open its heart, take valves out, fix 'em, put 'em back in, and when I finish, it works just like new. So how come I get such a small salary and you get loads of money when you and I are doing basically the same work?"

The surgeon paused, smiled and leaned over, and then whispered to the mechanic, "Try doing it with the engine running."

That'll be thirty guineas, please

A man goes to his doctor with a banana stuck in each ear and grapes stuck up his nose. He tells the doctor, "I feel terrible."

The doctor replies, "Of course you do – you're not eating properly."

Do you have it in pink?

A woman walks into a gun shop and asks the salesman if he can help her pick out a rifle.

"It's for my husband," she explains.

"Did he tell you what calibre to get?" asks the salesman.

"Are you kidding? He doesn't even know I'm going to shoot him."

The customer is always right

A man walks into a bank and says to the clerk, "I want to open a bloody account, you total, utter moron!"

"I'm sorry, sir?" says the clerk, taken aback.

"I said I want to open a bloody account, you dim-witted fool."

Offended by the attitude of the man, the clerk warns the customer that he doesn't have to put up with this sort of abuse and promptly leaves.

Returning with the manager, he explains the situation.

"Well, sir, it seems we have a problem," says the manager.

"You're right," says the man. "I've won 50 million quid and want to open an account with you."

"I see," says the manager looking at his clerk, "so it's this idiot here that's the problem then."

The geeks had a word for it

There was a young man who wanted to become a great writer. When asked to define 'great', he said, "I want to write stuff that people will react to on a truly emotional level – stuff that will make them cry and howl in pain and anger!"

He now works for Microsoft, writing error messages.

We come in peace for all mankind

A NASA crew destined for a moon landing was training near a Navajo Indian reservation. A Navajo elder asked if he could send a message to the moon with the astronauts. The NASA crew agreed, then called in a translator. The message said, "Watch out for these guys. They have come to steal your land."

Playing around

One day, a man came home early from work and was greeted by his wife dressed in very sexy lingerie and high heels.

"Tie me up," she purred, "and you can do anything you want."

So he tied her up and went golfing.

How do you know if a stoner's crashed into your house?
He's still there.

Investor in people

An office manager arrives at his department and sees an employee sitting behind his desk, totally stressed out.

He gives him a spot of advice: “I went home every afternoon for two weeks and had myself pampered by my wife. It was fantastic, and it really helped me. Maybe you should give it a try, too.”

Two weeks later, when the manager arrives at his department, he sees the same man happy and full of energy at his desk. The faxes are piling up, and the computer is running at full speed.

“Excellent,” says the manager, “I see you followed my advice.”

“I did,” answers the employee. “It was great! By the way, I didn’t know you had such a nice house!”

Gee, thanks

A woman rushes downstairs into the foyer of a large hotel and screams at the receptionist, “Check me out! I’m in a hurry!”

The receptionist eyes her up for a second and says, “Not bad, but your bum’s a bit big.”

What's the difference between a bad lawyer and a good lawyer?
A bad lawyer can let a case drag on for months. A good lawyer can make it last for years.

Living dangerously

A man walks into a pub with a neck brace, orders a pint and asks the landlord, "Who's in the lounge?"

The landlord replies, "There's 15 people playing darts."

The man says, "Get them a pint, too." Then he asks, "Who's upstairs?"

The landlord replies, "150 people at the disco."

The man says, "Get them pints too."

"That'll be £328, please," says the landlord.

The man replies, "Sorry, I haven't got that much money on me."

The landlord remarks, "If you were at the pub down the road, they'd have broken your neck."

"Just been there," says the man.

You got me there

One night, a policewoman pulls over a drunk driver. She asks him to step out of his car and says, "Anything you say can and will be held against you."

The drunk thinks about this for a moment and says, "Breasts."

How do you make a dog drink?
Put it in the liquidizer.

And make it snippy

A man visits his GP with a delicate matter: "I was thinking about getting a vasectomy."

"Well, that's a big decision," says the doctor. "Have you talked it over with your family?"

"Oh, yes," says the man. "They're in favour of it, 15 to seven."

What do you call an artist with brown fingers?
Picasso.

What's the difference between roast beef and pea soup?
Anyone can roast beef.

All mod cons

Proudly showing off his new apartment to some friends late one night, a drunk leads the way to his bedroom. When they get there, they see that there's a big brass gong taking pride of place.

"What's with that gong?" one of the friends asks.

"That's no gong," the drunk replies. "It's a talking clock!"

"Oh yeah? How does it work, then?" the friend asks.

"Watch," the drunk says. He moves to the corner of the room, picks up a hammer and pounds the gong as loudly as he can.

Suddenly, someone on the other side of the wall starts screaming, "What the hell do you think you're doing? It's three o'clock in the bloody morning!"

Why was the Energizer Bunny arrested?
He was charged with battery.

It never fails

A man walks into a pub and immediately spots a gorgeous woman standing at the bar. The man strides up to her and, by way of a chat-up line, says, "Do you want to see some magic?"

"What sort of magic?" the intrigued lady asks.

"You come back home with me, have sex and then disappear."

Life lesson

A little girl returns home from school and announces that a friend has told her where babies come from. Amused, her mother replies, "Why don't you tell me all about it?" The little girl explains, "Well, mummy and daddy take off all their clothes, and then daddy's thingy stands up, and then the mummy puts it in her mouth, and then it sort of explodes." Her mother shakes her head, leans over to meet her eye-to-eye, and says, "Oh, that's sweet, but that's not how you get babies. That's how you get jewellery."

Let's call it quits

A man who hates his wife's cat decides to get rid of it by driving it to the next town and leaving it there. But when he gets home, the cat's already back. The next day, he drops the cat off even further away, but the same thing happens. Finally, the man dumps the cat hundreds of miles away.

Hours later, the man calls home to his wife: "Honey, is the cat there?"

"Yes," she says.

"Can you put him on? I'm lost."

Did you hear about the new French tank?
It has 14 gears. Thirteen go in reverse and one forward, in case the enemy attacks from behind.

Last request

Two men were asked what they would like to be said about them at their funerals. The first one said, "I want someone to say I was the greatest footballer ever."

The other man said, "I want someone to say, 'He's moving, he's moving!'"

The divine plan

Three men are arguing in a pub. The first says, "God must be a mechanical engineer; just look at the joints in the human body." The second says, "God's an electrical engineer; look at the nervous system." The third says, "God has to be a civil engineer; who else would run a waste disposal pipeline through a perfectly good recreational area?"

A lump in the throat

A man goes to a barbershop for a shave. While the barber is lathering him up, he mentions the problems he has getting a close shave around the cheeks.

"I have just the thing," says the barber, taking a small wooden ball from a nearby drawer. "Just place this between your cheek and gum."

The man places the ball in his mouth and the barber proceeds with the closest shave the man has ever experienced.

After a few strokes, the client asks in garbled speech, "But what if I swallow it?"

"No problem," says the barber. "Just bring it back tomorrow like everyone else does."

New man

Three Aussies were working on a high-rise building project – Steve, Bruce and Bluey. Steve falls off and is killed instantly. As the ambulance takes the body away, Bruce says, "Someone should go and tell his wife."

Bluey says, "OK. I'm pretty good at that sensitive stuff, so let me do it."

Two hours later, he comes back carrying a crate of beer.

Bruce says, "Where did you get that from, Bluey?"

"Steve's wife gave it to me," Bluey replies.

"That's unbelievable," says Bruce. "You told the lady her husband was dead and she gave you the beer?"

"Well, not exactly," Bluey says. "When she answered the door, I said to her, 'You must be Steve's widow'. She said, 'I'm not a widow'. And I said, 'I'll bet you a crate of beer you are'."

What did the redneck say to his girlfriend after breaking up with her?
"Can we still be cousins?"

Did you hear about the guy in hospital for sniffing curry powder?
He's in a korma.

No wonder they made him the schoolteacher

The residents of a redneck town keep falling down a deep hole in the middle of its main street and always end up dying because the nearest hospital is located some 40 miles away. The mayor calls a town meeting to address the issue and asks for suggestions.

"We need our own hospital!" suggests one local.

"That's beyond our budget," answers the mayor. "Anyone else got any ideas?"

"I got a perfect idea," says another hick. "Just dig the hole next to the hospital."

A man walks into a record shop and asks, "What have you got by The Doors?"
The owner replies, "A mop and a fire extinguisher."

Two minds with but a single thought

During a boring blind date, a man takes a call from a friend. He leaves the table to answer it and decides it gives him an opportunity to escape. When he returns to his date he looks upset and says, "I'm afraid my grandad's just died. I must go."

"I understand," says the girl. "If yours hadn't died, mine would have had to."

Under the knife

Four surgeons took a coffee break and discussed their work. The first said, "I think accountants are the easiest to operate on. You open them up and everything inside is numbered."

The second said, "Librarians are easier. You open them up and everything is alphabeticised."

The third said, "I like to operate on electricians. You open them up and everything inside is colour-coded."

The fourth one said, "I like to operate on lawyers. They're heartless, spineless, gutless and their heads and their arses are interchangeable."

What did the Mexican fireman name his twins?
Hose A and Hose B.

Lead, kindly light

Two men meet while walking their dogs through a graveyard. One says to the other, "Morning."

The second man replies, "No, just walking the dog."

What goes, "Click. Is that it? Click. Is that it? Click. Is that it?"?
A blindfolded man doing a Rubik's Cube.

With friends like these

The Lone Ranger and Tonto are riding in the desert when hostile Apaches surround them.

The Lone Ranger turns to his trusted sidekick and says, "It looks like we're in trouble, old friend."

Tonto replies, "Who the hell are you, paleface?"

What do a farmer and a pimp have in common?
Both need a hoe to stay in business.

Law of the jungle

A missionary has spent years teaching agriculture and 'civilization' to some people in a distant land. One day, he wants to start teaching them English. So he takes the tribal chief and points at a tree.

"Tree," says the missionary.

"Tree," mimics the chief.

The holy man then points to a rock.

"Rock," he says.

"Rock," copies the chief.

All of a sudden, they come upon two people having sex in the bushes. Embarrassed, the missionary blurts out that they are 'riding a bike'. Then the chief pulls out his blowpipe and shoots the two people.

"What are you doing?" yells the missionary. "I've spent all this time civilizing you, and you turn around and do this!"

"My bike," says the chief.

What's the last thing a drummer says before leaving a band?
"Why don't we try one of my songs?"

Why was the pasty in the pub?
He was meetin' potato.

We've all got to go some time

A man goes to his doctor for a complete check-up. Afterwards, the doctor comes out with the results. "I'm afraid I have some bad news," says the doctor. "You don't have much time."

"Oh, no, that's terrible. How long have I got?" the man asks.

"Ten," says the doctor.

"Ten what? Months? Weeks?"

"Nine..." continues the doctor.

What do you call a lawyer with an IQ of 50?
Your Honour.

That stuff goes right through you

A skeleton walks into a bar. The barman asks, "What can I get you?" The skeleton replies, "I'll have a pint of lager and a mop, please."

Just a nip

A man walking down the street sees a woman with perfect breasts. He says to her, “Excuse me, miss, but would you let me bite your breasts for £100?”

“Are you mad?” she replies, and keeps walking. He turns around, runs around the block and gets to the corner before she does.

“Would you let me bite your breasts for £1,000?” he asks again.

“Listen, you, I’m not that kind of woman! Got it?” The man will not give up and catches up with her again. “OK, final offer. Would you let me bite your breasts, just once, for £10,000?”

She thinks about it for a while and says, “£10,000, eh? OK, just once.”

She takes off her blouse to reveal the most perfect breasts in the world. As soon as he sees them, he grabs them and starts caressing them, fondling them slowly, kissing them and burying his face in them, but not biting them. The woman finally gets annoyed and asks, “Well? Are you going to bite them or not?”

“Nah,” he replies. “Too expensive.”

What do you call a guy born in Leeds, who grows up in Edinburgh and dies in Liverpool?
Dead.

We have lift-off

Dave and Jim worked as aeroplane mechanics in London. One day, the airport was fogbound and they were stuck in the hangar. Dave said, "I wish we had a drink."

"Me, too." replied Jim. "Y'know, I've heard you can drink jet fuel and get a buzz. You want to try it?" So they poured themselves a couple of glasses and got completely smashed.

The next morning, Dave woke up and was surprised at how good he felt. Then the phone rang and it was Jim. "Hey, how do you feel this morning?" he asked.

"I feel great," said Dave. "How about you?"

"I feel great, too." Jim responded. "Have you broken wind yet?"

"No," said Dave.

"Well, don't – I'm in Glasgow!"

What do you get when you cross LSD with a birth control pill?
A trip without the kids.

Boom-boom!

Three blokes with dogs walk into a pub. The first orders a bottle of beer and, when it comes, his dog pours it for him. The second orders a beer, and his dog opens some crisps. The third orders a beer but, when it comes, his dog just sits there.

"Your dog doesn't do any tricks?" asks the first guy.

"He's a blacksmith," says the third.

"What do you mean?"

"If you pour beer over him, he'll make a bolt for the door."

What's grey, eats fish and lives in Washington DC?
The Presidential Seal.

What do you call a judge with no thumbs?
Justice Fingers.

Miss! Miss!

A customer wanted to ask his attractive waitress for a date but couldn't get her attention. When he was finally able to catch her eye, she quickly looked away.

Finally, he followed her into the kitchen and blurted out his invitation. To his amazement, she said yes. So he asked, "Why have you been avoiding me all this time? You wouldn't even make eye contact with me."

"Oh," replied the waitress, "I just thought you were after more coffee."

What's the difference between a waitress who works in a strip club and a stripper?
Two weeks.

God sees all

During his wedding rehearsal, the groom approached the vicar and said, “Look, I’ll give you £100 if you’ll change the wedding vows and miss out the ‘love, honour and obey’ part.”

He passed the clergyman the cash and left the church satisfied.

On his wedding day, when it came time for the groom’s vows, the vicar looked the young man in the eye and said: “Will you promise to love, honour and obey her every command and wish, serve her breakfast in bed every morning and swear that you will never look at another woman, as long as you both shall live?”

The groom gulped and said in a squeaky voice, “Yes.”

He then leaned toward the vicar and hissed through clenched teeth, “I thought we had a deal?”

The vicar looked at the bride. “She made me a better offer.”

What’s the punishment for bigamy?
Two mothers-in-law.

Why don't women blink during foreplay?
They don't have time.

Second opinion

A beautiful woman about to undergo a minor operation is lying on a trolley in a hospital corridor awaiting the doctors.

A man in a white coat approaches, lifts up the sheet and examines her naked body. He walks away and confers with another man in a white coat. He approaches and does the same thing.

When a third man approaches her, she asks impatiently, "These examinations are fine, but when are you going to start the operation?"

He shrugs and says, "Your guess is as good as mine, lady. We're just here to paint the corridor."

Great puns of our time no. 94

Saint George went to a transvestite party and said: "How do you like me with my drag on?"

What do you call a large cloud that marries lots of smaller clouds?
A bigger mist.

Telling it straight

A teacher says to her class, “I’m going to call on each of you and you’re going to tell me what your father does for a living. Tommy, you’re first.”

Tommy says, “My father’s a doctor.”

The teacher says, “Jamie, what about you?”

Jamie says, “My father’s a lawyer.”

Finally, there’s one boy left and the teacher says, “Billy, what does your father do?”

Billy replies, “My father’s dead, Miss.”

Shocked, the teacher says, “I’m so sorry. What did he do before he died?”

Billy says, “He turned purple and collapsed on the dog, Miss.”

How many men do you need for a Mafia funeral?
Just one. To slam the car boot shut.

Be sure your sins will find you out

A man spent days looking for his wallet. Finally, he decided that he'd go to church and steal one from one of the many jackets left in the cloakroom.

The would-be thief went to church and sat at the back. The sermon was about the Ten Commandments, but instead of sneaking out he waited until the sermon was over and went to talk to the vicar.

"Father, I came here today to steal a wallet, but after hearing your sermon, I changed my mind."

The delighted man of God said, "Bless you, my son. Was it when I preached, 'Thou shall not steal' that you had a change of heart?"

The man responded, "No, it was the one about adultery. When you started to preach about that, I suddenly remembered where I left my wallet."

What did the German clockmaker say to the clock that only went, "Tick, tick, tick"?
"Ve haff vays of making you tock!"

In the number two shirt

Sven-Goran Eriksson walks into the changing room after a particularly vigorous training session – only to spot a steaming turd on the floor.

Fuming, the Swede looks at his players and bawls, "Who's sh*t on the floor?"

"Me, boss," cries Peter Crouch, "but I'm not too bad in the air."

Do you know how copper wire was invented?
Two lawyers were fighting over a penny.

Long odds

A 90-year-old man says to his doctor, "I have an 18-year-old bride who's pregnant with my child. What do you think of that?"

The doctor says, "I have an elderly friend who's a hunter. One day, when he was going out in a hurry, he accidentally picked up his umbrella instead of his gun. When he got to the field, he saw a rabbit sitting beside the stream. He raised his umbrella and went, 'Bang, bang' and the rabbit fell dead. What do you think of that?"

The 90-year-old says, "I'd say somebody else killed that rabbit."

The doctor replies, "My point exactly."

What did the mother turkey say to her disobedient children?
"If your father could see you now, he'd turn in his gravy."

Thanks anyway

A man was walking down the street in a sweat because he had an important meeting and couldn't find a parking space.

Looking up towards Heaven he said, "Lord, take pity on me. If you can find me a parking space, I'll go to church every Sunday for the rest of my life and give up lager."

Miraculously, a parking space appeared.

The man looked up to Heaven again and said, "Never mind – I found one."

Why do police have trouble solving murders by rednecks?
Because they all have the same DNA.

Can't I just walk along a line?

A driver was pulled over by a policeman for speeding.

As the officer was writing the ticket, he noticed several machetes in the car. "What are those for?" he asked suspiciously. "I'm a juggler," the man replied. "I use those in my act." "Well, show me," the officer demanded.

The driver got out the machetes and started juggling them, eventually doing seven at one time. Seeing this, the driver of another car passing by said to his passenger, "Remind me never to drink and drive. Look at the test they're giving now."

Right back atcha

A guy returns home one day and says to his girlfriend, "Look, I've bought the new Oasis CD."

"Why did you do that?" the girlfriend laughs. "We don't even have a CD player!"

"So what?" says the chap. "Have I ever asked why you keep buying bras?"

What is it that separates five nymphomaniacs from two drunks?
The cockpit door.

Making dough

The owner of a family-run bakery was being questioned by the Inland Revenue about his tax return, having reported a net profit of £45,000 for the year.

"Why don't you people leave me alone?" the baker said. "I work like a dog, everyone in my family helps out and the place is only closed three days a year. And you want to know how I made £45,000?"

"It's not your income that bothers us," the taxman said. "It's these deductions. You listed six trips to Bermuda for you and your wife."

"Oh, that?" the owner said, smiling. "I forgot to tell you – we also deliver."

Why do Rover cars have heated rear windows?
To keep your hands warm while you're pushing.

What do you call an Aussie farmer with a sheep under each arm?
A pimp.

One size fits all

One day, two old ladies are sitting outside their nursing home having a cigarette when it starts to rain. One of the old ladies whips out a condom, cuts the end off, puts it over her cigarette and continues smoking.

Maude: "What the hell is that?"

Mabel: "A condom. This way my cigarette doesn't get wet."

Maude: "Where did you get it?"

Mabel: "You can get them at any chemist."

The next day, Maude hobbles down to her local pharmacy and announces to the chemist that she wants a box of condoms. Obviously embarrassed, he looks at her, but very delicately asks what brand she would prefer.

Maude: "Doesn't matter, as long as it fits on a Camel."

A man goes to the zoo but when he arrives there's only a dog.
It was a shih-tzu.

And they're off!

Riding the favourite at Cheltenham, a jockey is well ahead of the field. Suddenly, he is hit on the head by a turkey and a string of sausages.

He manages to stay on his mount and pull back into the lead, only to be struck by a box of Christmas crackers and a dozen mince pies over the last fence.

He again manages to regain the lead when he's hit by a bottle of sherry full in the face.

Eventually, he comes in second. Furious, he goes to the stewards' room to complain that he has been seriously hampered.

What do you call a woman who works as hard as a man?
Lazy.

Heap big pun

An Indian chief had three wives, each of whom was pregnant. The first gave birth to a boy and the chief was so elated he built her a teepee made of deerhide.

A few days later the second gave birth, also to a boy. The chief was very happy and he built her a teepee made of antelope hide.

The third wife gave birth a few days later, but the chief kept the details a secret. He built this one a two-storey teepee, using hippopotamus hide. The chief then challenged the tribe to guess what had occurred.

Many tried and failed. Finally, one young brave declared that the third wife gave birth to twin boys.

"Correct," said the chief. "How did you figure it out?"

The brave replied, "It's elementary, really – the value of the squaw of the hippopotamus is equal to the sons of the squaws of the other two hides."

How many drinkers does it take to change a light bulb?
Never mind. We'll drink in the dark.

Getting technical

One day at school, a teacher asks her class to write a sentence about a public servant, and little Jonny writes, "The fireman came down the ladder pregnant."

When she gets around to marking Jonny's answer, the teacher takes him aside to correct him. "Don't you know what pregnant means?" she asks.

"Sure," says Jonny. "It means carrying a child."

Why did the chicken cross the playground?
To get to the other slide.

That's my boy!

Two old men are arguing about whose dog is smarter.

"My dog's practically a genius," the first fella boasts. "Every morning he waits patiently for the newspaper to be delivered and then brings it in to me."

"I know," the second fella replies.

"What do you mean?" the first man asks. "How do you know?"

The second man answers, "My dog told me about it."

Your sins are forgiven you

A nun goes to confession. "Forgive me, Father," she says. "I used horrible language this weekend."

"Go on," the priest says.

"Well," the nun continues, "I was playing golf and hit an incredible drive, but it hit a phone line and fell short after about only 100 yards."

"And you swore?" the priest asks.

"No," the nun says. "After that, a squirrel ran out and stole my ball."

"You swore then?" the priest asks.

"Well, no," the nun says. "Then, an eagle swooped down and grabbed the squirrel in his talons. As they flew away, the squirrel dropped my ball."

"Then you swore?" the father asks.

"No," she continues. "The ball fell on a big rock, rolled on to the green and stopped six inches from the hole."

The priest is silent for a moment and then finally says, "You missed the f**king putt, didn't you?"

Revenge is sweet

There are two statues in a park, one of a nude man and one of a nude woman. They had been facing each other across a pathway for a hundred years when one day an angel comes down from the sky and, with a single gesture, brings the two to life. "As a reward for being so patient," says the angel, "you have been given life for 30 minutes to do what you've wished to do the most." Immediately, the two statues disappear off behind a shrubbery. The angel waits patiently as the bushes rustle and giggling ensues until, after fifteen minutes, the two return out of breath. The angel tells them, "Um, you have fifteen minutes left."

The male statue asks the female statue, "Shall we do it again?"

"Oh, yes," she replies. "But let's change positions. This time, I'll hold the pigeon down, and you crap on its head."

What do you get when you have 32 rednecks in a room?
A full set of teeth.

A lucky escape

A man walks into a bar grinning his face off. "The beers are on me!" he says, happily. "My wife has just run off with my best friend."

"That's a shame," says the barman. "Why aren't you sad?"

"Sad?" asks the man. "They've saved me a fortune. They were both pregnant."

For God and country

A famous Welsh footballer died and upon arriving at the Pearly Gates was asked by the angel waiting for him, "Do you know of any reason why you should not enter the kingdom of Heaven?"

"Well," said the footballer, "once I was playing for Wales against England and I used my hand to push the ball past an English defender. The ref never saw it and I went on to score."

"Ah, that's OK," said the angel. "We can let you in."

"Oh, great!" replied the footballer. "That's been on my mind for ages. Thanks, Saint Peter!"

"That's OK," said the angel. "Oh, and by the way, boyo, Saint Peter's off today – I'm Saint David."

VIP treatment

The Pope lands in New York Airport, where a limo is waiting for him. The Pope gets in and says to the limo driver, "Mate, I haven't got a lot left in me. Please may I have an opportunity to drive a limo before I leave this world?" The limo driver thinks about it and agrees. The Pope then proceeds to drive the limo at 105mph down the streets of Manhattan until he's stopped by the police. The Pope winds down the window and gives the usual "Sorry, officer, I didn't know I was speeding" spiel. The cop gets on his radio and calls head office.

"I've pulled over a limo for speeding and it's got a very important passenger," says the cop.

"Who is it? The senator? The president?" asks the commissioner.

"No, much more important than that," replies the cop.

"Who's more important than the president?" scoffs the commissioner.

"I think it's God," says the cop.

"How could it possibly be God, you fool?" asks the commissioner.

"Well," replies the cop. "The Pope is the chauffeur."

Another time, maybe

An executive was in a quandary. He had to get rid of one of his staff and had narrowed it down to one of two people – Deborah or Jack. It would be a hard decision to make, as they were both equally qualified and both did excellent work, but finally he made his decision.

He approaches Deborah by the water cooler and says, "Deborah, I've never done this before, but I have to lay you or Jack off."

"Could you jack off," she replies. "I've got a rotten headache."

I'll rephrase that

Two American women, one from the north and one from the deep south, are seated next to one another on a plane.

"Where you flyin' to?" asks the redneck, to which the northern woman turns up her nose.

"Don't you know you should never end a sentence with a preposition?" she says.

The southern woman thinks about this for a second.

"OK, where you flyin' to, bitch?"

"My wife is an angel."
"Lucky you. Mine's still alive."

Stating the obvious

A couple were on a driving holiday through deepest Wales, and passed through the town named Llanfairpwllgwyngyllgo gerychwyrndrobwllllantysiliogogogoch. They were obviously having trouble trying to say the word and neither really knew the correct Welsh pronunciation, so they decided to stop for lunch in the town and maybe ask a local how to say the name properly. As they sat in the restaurant, the husband leaned over to talk to a young blonde girl sitting at the next table. "Excuse me," said the man. "We were wondering if you could tell us the name of where we are. Could you pronounce it really slowly?" The young blonde looked at the man in a slightly bemused way, then leaned over towards him and said, "Burrrrrr... Gurrrrrr... Kiiiiiinnng."

What was the last thing Nelson said to his men before they got on the boat?
"Get on the boat."

Die happy

A bloke working in a brewery died one day after falling into a vat of beer, and it was the managing director's duty to inform his widow. "Tell me," cried the widow. "Did he suffer much?"

"I don't think so," replied the MD. "He got out to go to the toilet about three times."

For whom the bells toll

Twelve priests were about to be ordained. The final test was for them to line up in a row, totally nude, while a sexy, big-breasted model danced before them. Each priest had a small bell attached to their penis and were told that anyone whose bell rang would not be ordained because he had not reached a state of spiritual purity. Eventually, the beautiful model danced before the first candidate, with no reaction. She proceeded down the line with the same response from all the priests until she got to the final priest, called Carlos. As she danced, his bell began to ring so loudly that it flew off and fell clattering to the ground. Embarrassed, Carlos took a few steps forward and bent over to pick it up. Then, all at once, the other bells started to ring.

Did you hear about the dyslexic pimp?
He bought a warehouse.

The painful truth

A man goes to the dentist and asks how much it is for a tooth extraction. "£85 for an extraction, sir," was the dentist's reply.

"Have you not got anything cheaper?" replied the man, getting agitated. "But that's the normal charge for an extraction, sir," said the dentist. "What if I don't use any anaesthetic?" asked the man, hopefully. "Well, it's highly unusual, sir, but if that's what you want, I suppose I can do it for £60," said the dentist. "Hmm, what about if you used one of your dental trainees and still without any anaesthetic?" asked the man. "Well, it's possible, but it'll be a lot more painful. If that was the case we could bring the price down to, say, £30," said the dentist. "What if you use it as part of a student training session?" the man asked. "Hmm, well, OK... it'll be good for the students, I suppose. I'll charge you only £5 in that case," said the dentist. "OK, now you're talking. It's a deal!" said the man. "Can you confirm an appointment next Tuesday for the wife?"

I confess

Henry goes to confession and says, “Bless me, Father, for I have sinned. Last night I was with seven different women.”

The priest quietly replies, “Take seven lemons, squeeze them into a glass and drink the juice without pausing.”

Henry, looking surprised, says, “Will that cleanse me of my sins, Father?”

“No,” says the priest. “But it’ll wipe that stupid grin off your face.”

A policeman got out of his car and the lad who was stopped for speeding rolled down his window. “I’ve been waiting for you all day,” the policeman said. “Yeah,” replied the lad. “Well, I got here as fast as I could.”

Now you see it...

A young magician got a job working on a cruise ship with his pet parrot. The parrot would always ruin his act by saying things like, "He has a card up his sleeve," or "He has a dove in his pocket." One day the ship sank and the magician and the parrot found themselves alone on a lifeboat. For a couple of days, they just sat there looking at each other. Finally, the parrot broke the silence and said, "OK, I give up. What did you do with the ship?"

A man goes into the barbers. The barber asks, "Do you want a crew cut?"
The man replies, "No, thanks, it's just for me."

Say it with flowers

A woman sent flowers to someone who was moving to Spain for a job promotion. She also sent flowers the same day to a funeral for a friend. Later, she found that the flower shop had got the cards mixed up. The man who was moving received the card that said, "Deepest condolences," and the card they sent to the funeral home said, "I know it's hot where you're going, but you deserve it."

The right career move

A plumber attended to a leaking tap at a stately home. After a two-minute job, he demanded £75. “Christ, even I don’t charge this much and I’m a surgeon!” said the owner.

The plumber replied, “You’re right – that’s why I switched from surgery to plumbing.”

Chaos theory

A doctor, an engineer, a vicar and a Royal Mail postman were debating who was the world’s first professional. The doctor said, “It must have been a doctor. Who else could have helped with the world’s first surgery of taking a rib from Adam to make Eve, the first woman?”

“No,” said the vicar. “It must have been a rabbi, since the Lord needed someone to help preach his message to Adam and the world.”

“Wait,” said the engineer. “The world was created in six days from nothing. Do you know what a master engineering feat that must have been to create the whole world into an organised, civilised place from utter chaos?”

“Yes, but who created the chaos?” asked the Royal Mail man.

One morning A man phones up his work and says to his boss, "Sorry, but I can't come in today, I'm feeling a little sick."
The boss asks, "What do you mean 'a little sick'? Just how sick are you?"
The man replies, "Well, I've just had sex with my dog."

Taking a dive

One day, a diver is enjoying the aquatic world 20 feet below the sea's surface when he notices a bloke at the same depth, but with no scuba gear whatsoever. The diver goes down another 20 feet and, after a few minutes, the bloke joins him. The diver goes down 25 feet more and, minutes later, the same bloke joins him again.

This confuses the diver, so he takes out a waterproof chalkboard set and writes, "How the hell are you able to stay this deep under water without breathing apparatus?"

The other guy grabs the board, erases what the diver has written, and scribbles, "I'm drowning, you bloody moron!"

What do you call a New Zealander with a sheep under one arm and a goat under the other? Bisexual.

A helping hand

The Prime Minister was out walking on a beautiful snowy day, when he saw that somebody had urinated on the Downing Street lawn to spell out "The PM is a d*ckhead". Infuriated, he called on the secret service to figure out who had done it. In a few hours, they came to him and told him that there was some bad news and some worse news.

"The bad news is that the urine is from the Chancellor."

"Al? How could he do this to me? What could be worse than this?"

"The handwriting is your wife's."

A woman went into a hardware shop to buy an axe. "It's for my husband," she told the assistant. "Did he tell you what poundage he was after?" asked the guy.
"Are you joking?" she asked. "He doesn't even know I'm going to kill him!"

Two lawyers are walking down the street, when a beautiful woman walks by. "Boy, I'd like to screw her," says one lawyer.
"Yeah, I would, too," says the other. "But out of what?"

It's in the bag

A cowboy walks into a bar and orders a whiskey. When the bartender delivers the drink, the cowboy asks, "Where is everybody?" The bartender replies, "They've gone to the hanging." "Hanging? Who are they hanging?" "Brown Paper Pete," the bartender replies. "What kind of a name is that?" the cowboy asks. "Well," says the bartender. "He wears a brown paper hat, brown paper shirt, brown paper trousers and brown paper shoes." "How bizarre," says the cowboy. "What are they hanging him for?" "Rustling," says the bartender.

It's the morning after the honeymoon and the wife says, "You know something, you really are a lousy lover."
The husband replies, "How can you tell after only 30 seconds?"

Why are the English better lovers than the French?
Because only an Englishman could stay on top for 90 minutes and still finish second.

The simple answer

A boy comes home from school and says to his dad, "Dad, what's the difference between 'potentially' and 'realistically'?" His dad says, "Son, go and ask your mum if she'll sleep with Robert Redford for one million pounds, then go and ask your sister if she'll sleep with Brad Pitt for one million pounds." The boy says to his mum, "Mum, would you sleep with Robert Redford for one million pounds?" "Definitely," she replies. He then says to his sister, "Sarah, would you sleep with Brad Pitt for one million pounds?" "Definitely," she replies. The boy then returns to his dad, who says, "Did you find out the difference?" The boy replies, "Yes, potentially we are sitting on two million quid, realistically we are living with a couple of slappers."

What would life be like without women?
A real pain in the arse.

It's a family affair

One Sunday morning, George burst into the living room and said, "Dad! Mum! I have some great news for you! I am getting married to the most beautiful girl in town, and her name is Susan." After dinner, George's dad took him aside. "Son, I have to talk with you. Your mother and I have been married 30 years and she's a wonderful wife... but she has never offered much excitement in the bedroom, so I used to fool around with other women a lot. Susan is actually your half-sister, and I'm afraid you can't marry her." George was broken-hearted. After eight months, he eventually started dating girls again. A year later he came home and very proudly announced, "Diane said yes! We're getting married in June." Again, his father insisted on another private conversation, and broke the sad news: "Diane is your half-sister too, George. I'm awfully sorry about this." George was livid! He finally decided to tell his mother the truth about his father. "Dad has done so much harm. I guess I'm never going to get married," he complained. "Every time I fall in love, Dad tells me the girl is my half-sister."

"Don't worry about that," his mother chuckled, shaking her head. "He's not really your father."

Woman: "Can I get Viagra here?"
Pharmacist: "Yes."
Woman: "Can I get it over the counter?"
Pharmacist: "If you give me two of them, you can."

Mission accomplished

A man was knocking back the drinks in a bar. "I think you've had enough, mate," said the barman. "But I've just lost my wife," slurred the drunk indignantly. The barman said sympathetically: "Well, it must be hard losing a wife." The man replied, "Hard? It was almost impossible."

Robbie Williams and Emile Heskey are on a sinking ship. Who gets saved?
The music world and Birmingham City.

Not on my job description

An old woman is on a plane and is getting increasingly worried about the turbulence around her. She turns to the vicar next to her and asks: "Reverend, you are a man of God. Why can't you do something about this problem?"

"Lady," says the vicar. "I'm in sales, not management."

Some you win...

A big Texan cowboy stopped at a local restaurant after a day of drinking and roaming around in Mexico. While sipping his tequila, he noticed a sizzling, scrumptious-looking platter being served at the next table. Not only did it look good, but the smell was wonderful. He asked the waiter, "What is that you just served?" The waiter replied: "Ah, señor, you have excellent taste! Those are bull's testicles from the bullfight this morning. A delicacy! But there is only one serving per day. If you come early tomorrow and place your order, we will be sure to save you this delicacy!" The next morning, the cowboy returned, placed his order, and then that evening he was served the one and only portion of the special delicacy of the day. After a few bites, and inspecting the contents of his platter, he called to the waiter and said, "These are delicious, but they are much, much smaller than the ones I saw you serve yesterday." The waiter shrugged his shoulders and replied, "Si, señor. Sometimes the bull wins."

How many psychiatrists does it take to change a light bulb?
Only one, but it really has to want to change.

A man asked a waiter: "I'm just wondering, exactly how do you prepare your chickens?"
"Nothing special, sir. We just tell them straight out that they're going to die."

The name escapes me

A man walks into a pub with his wife. His wife sits down while he orders drinks and a friend of his at the bar asks him where he's been.

"On holiday," he replies.

"Where on holiday?" his friend asks.

"Spain."

"Whereabouts in Spain?"

"Some little village on the coast."

"What's it called?"

"I forget. What's the name of that plant that grows up the sides of houses?"

"Ivy."

"That's it," he says. "Ivy, what's the name of the village we stayed at in Spain?"

Lost in translation

Two Mexicans have been lost in the desert for weeks. At death's door, they see a tree in the distance. As they get nearer, they see that it's draped with rasher upon rasher of bacon: smoked bacon, crispy bacon, juicy bacon, all sorts of bacon. "Hey, Pepe," says the first Mexican, "ees a bacon tree! We're saved!" So Pepe goes on ahead and runs up to the tree. As he gets to within five feet of it, he's gunned down in a hail of bullets. His friend drops down on the sand and yells across to the dying man: "Pepe! Pepe! Que pasa, hombre?" With his last breath Pepe calls out, "Ugh, run, amigo, run – ees not a bacon tree, ees a ham bush."

What's brown and black and looks good on a lawyer?
A doberman.

Thin-skinned

A young polar bear walks up to his dad one day and asks: "Dad, am I a pure polar bear? You know, not part black bear or grizzly bear or anything?" "Why no, son. You come from a long line of proud and strong polar bears. Why do you ask?" "Because I'm f**king cold."

Be careful what you wish for

Two men were out fishing, when they found a lamp floating in the water. One of the men picked it up and rubbed it, and straight away a genie appeared from the lamp. Unfortunately, it was a very low-level genie, and could only grant one wish. The men thought for a few minutes and then wished for the entire lake to be made of the best beer in the world. With a flash the wish was granted. All of a sudden, one of the men got really angry. “Dammit! Now we have to piss in the boat!”

An apple a day...

A young man asked an old rich man how he made his money. The old guy stroked his worsted wool vest and said, “Well, son, it was 1932 – the depth of the Great Depression. I was down to my last penny so I invested it in an apple. I spent the entire day polishing the apple and, at the end of the day, I sold it for two pence. The next morning, I invested those two pence in two apples. I spent the entire day polishing them and sold them at 5pm for 4p. I continued this system for a month, by the end of which I’d accumulated a fortune of £1.35. Then my wife’s father died and left us two million pounds.”

Watch what you eat

Two men are sitting in the doctor's office. The first man is holding his shoulder in pain, while the second man has ketchup in his hair, fried egg down the front of his shirt and two sausages sticking out of his pockets. After a while, the second man asks the other what happened. "My cat got stuck in a tree," the man says, gripping his arm. I went up after him and fell out. I think I've broken my shoulder. You?"

"Oh, it's nothing serious," the second man replies. "I'm just not eating properly."

It doesn't quite add up

A bank manager in America notices that one of his new cashiers lacks basic arithmetic skills. He calls the new man into his office. "Son, where did you say you studied finance again?" the manager asks.

"Yale, sir," the cashier replies.

"I see," says the bank manager, certain he must have pulled the wrong employee aside. "And what did you say your name was?"

"Yim Yohnson, sir," he replies.

After surgery, a man wakes up drowsily in the hospital. He yells to the nurse, "I can't feel my legs!"
"Well, of course you can't," she replies. "You have just had your arms amputated."

Turn a deaf ear

A policeman in a small town stopped a motorist who was speeding down the High Street. "But, officer," the man began, "I can explain."

"Quiet!" snapped the officer. "I'm going to let you spend the night in jail until the sergeant gets back."

"But, officer, I just wanted to say..."

"I said be quiet! You're going to jail!"

A few hours later the officer looked in on his prisoner and said, "Lucky for you, the sarge is at his daughter's wedding so he'll be in a good mood when he gets back."

"Don't count on it," answered the bloke in the cell. "I'm the groom."

Why did the blonde take a ladder into the bar?
She heard the drinks were on the house.

A nine-year-old boy walks into a bar and demands the barmaid give him a Scotch on the rocks.
"Hey, do you want to get me into trouble?" the barmaid asks.
"Maybe later," says the kid, "but for now I'll just have my drink."

Record breaker

A man walks into a music store to buy an old-school LP. As he gets ready to pay, he discovers that he has forgotten his wallet. But instead of running home to get it, he decides to steal the record by putting it down his pants. The cashier spots him on the way out and yells, "Hey! Is that a record in your pants?"

The man replies, "Well, I don't know if it's a record but I haven't heard of any complaints."

It's enough to wake the dead!

A funeral service is being held for a woman who has just died. As the pallbearers are carrying out the casket, they accidentally bump into a wall. Hearing a faint moan from inside, the woman's husband opens the casket to find that his wife is actually alive! She dies again ten years later and her husband has to arrange another funeral. This time, when the casket is carried towards the door, the husband yells, "Watch out for the bloody wall!"

The good news: Saddam Hussein is facing the death penalty.
The bad news: Beckham is taking it...

A fate worse than death

An Englishman, a Frenchman and a German survive a plane crash. They are stranded on a desert island and, knowing that nothing but certain death is to be their fate, God grants them one last wish. The Frenchman asks for a huge, sumptuous dinner washed down with an excellent Burgundy; the German asks if he can make the after-dinner speech; and the Englishman clasps his hands together and says: "Please, God, let me die before the German starts."

Did you hear about the dogs' home that got broken into?
The police still have no leads.

What was the question?

A man buys a 12 pack of condoms with his girlfriend and gets down to business straight away. A few days later, the two are at it again, and the woman realises that there are only three condoms left. A little confused, she confronts the man as to where the other condoms have gone. "I was masturbating," he replies. The girlfriend looks confused and says, "I've never heard of that." The next day she asks a male friend if he does the same, to which he replies, "Yeah, of course." The woman shrieks back, "Really? You've masturbated with a condom?" The man looks surprised and says, "Oh no, sorry. I thought you said have I ever cheated on my girlfriend."

Two prostitutes after the Christmas holidays.
"What did you ask Santa Claus to give you?" asks one.
"Hundred quid, as usual," replies the other.

Get it off your chest

An old couple were sitting on the porch one afternoon, rocking in their rocking chairs. All of a sudden, the old man reaches over and slaps his wife. "What was that for?" she asks. "That's for 40 years of rotten sex!" he replies. His wife doesn't say anything, and they start rocking again. All of a sudden, the old lady reaches over and slaps her husband hard across the face. "Well, what was that for?" he asks. "That's for knowing the difference!"

Honesty isn't always the best policy

Bob is sitting at the coffee shop, staring morosely into his cappuccino. Tom walks in and sits down. After trying to start a conversation several times and getting only distracted grunts, he asks Bob what the problem is.

"Well," says Bob, "I think I've upset my wife after she asked me one of those questions she always asks. Now I'm in deep trouble at home."

"What kind of question was it?"

"Well, my wife asked me if I would still love her when she was old, fat and ugly."

"That's easy," said Tom. "You just say, 'Of course I will!'"

"Yeah," said Bob, "that's what I did. Except I said, 'Of course I do.'"

Wise words

The teacher had given her class an assignment. She'd asked her pupils to get their parents to tell them a story that had a moral at the end of it. "So what have you got for me, Johnny?" she asks one pupil sitting at the back of the class.

"Well," replies Johnny. "My mum told a story about my dad. Dad was a pilot in Desert Storm, and his plane got hit. He had to bail out over enemy territory, and all he had was a small flask of whiskey, a pistol and a survival knife. He drank the whiskey on the way down, so it wouldn't fall into enemy hands, and then his parachute landed right in the middle of 20 enemy troops. He shot 15 of them with the gun, until he ran out of bullets, killed four more with the knife, until the blade broke, and then he killed the last one with his bare hands."

"Good heavens!" said the horrified teacher. "What kind of moral did your mum teach you from that horrible story?" The boy replied: "Stay the hell away from Dad when he's been drinking."

What is the worst thing that can happen to a bat while asleep?
The runs.

What has four legs and an arm?
A happy rottweiler.

One to tell the lads

A guy is shipwrecked on a celebrity cruise and wakes up stranded on a desert island with Kelly Brook. Anyway, after a few weeks they are having passionate sex. This is all fine and dandy for a bit, but the guy starts getting a bit depressed. Kelly comes up to him on the beach one day and asks, "What's the matter?"

"Well, it's wonderful," says the guy. "I'm on a tropical island with a beautiful woman, but... I miss my mates and going to the pub with them."

So Kelly replies, "Well, I'm an actress. Maybe if I get dressed in some of those male clothes which were left behind in the trunks, I can pretend to be one of your mates down the pub."

It sounded a bit weird but he thought he'd give it a try. So Kelly gets into the male clothing and they sit down next to each other. Then the guy goes, "Hey, Joe, you'll never guess who I've been shagging."

Wrong number

A young man joins a big corporate empire as a trainee. On his very first day at work, he dials the canteen and shouts into the phone, "Get me a coffee, quickly!"

The voice from the other side responds, "You fool, you've dialled the wrong extension. Do you know who you're talking to?"

The trainee goes white and says, "No, who is it?"

The voice on the end of the line continues, "It's the company CEO."

The trainee thinks for a moment and shouts back, "And do you know who you're talking to, you fool?"

"No," replies the CEO, indignantly.

"Good," says the trainee, and slams down the phone.

What do politicians do when they die?
Lie, still!

Thinking on your feet

A woman was having a passionate affair with an inspector from a pest-control company. One afternoon they were carrying on in the bedroom together when her husband arrived home quite unexpectedly. "Quick," said the woman to her lover. "Into the wardrobe!" And with that she pushed him into the wardrobe, stark naked. The husband, however, became suspicious and, after a search of the bedroom, discovered the man in the closet. "Who are you?" he asked him, with a snarl.

"I'm an inspector from Bugs-B-Gone," said the exterminator.

"What are you doing in there?" the husband asked.

"I'm investigating a complaint about moths," the man replied.

"So where are your clothes?" asked the husband.

The man looked down at himself and said, "Those little bastards."

Slow on the uptake

Two turtles are camping. After four days hiking, they realise they've left behind a bottle opener for their beer.

The first turns to the second and says, "You've got to go back or else we've got no lager." "No way," says the second turtle. "By the time I get back you'll have eaten all the food." The first turtle replies, "I promise I won't, OK? Just hurry."

Nine full days pass and there's still no sign of the second turtle, so the first finally cracks and digs into a sandwich. Suddenly the second turtle pops out from behind a rock and yells, "I knew it! I'm definitely not going now!"

Not for want of trying

An 85-year-old man visits his doctor to get a sperm count. The old fella's given a jar and told to bring back a sample. The next day he returns with an empty jar.

"What happened?" asks the doc.

"Well," the old man starts. "I asked my wife for help and she tried with her right hand and then with her left. Anyway, we got nothing. Then she tried with her mouth, first with her teeth in, then with her teeth out. Still nothing. We even called Evelyn, the lady next door, but still nothing."

The doctor bursts out, "You asked your neighbour?!"

So the old man replies, "Yep, no matter what we tried, we couldn't get that damn jar open."

Food for thought

Two best friends crash their plane in a desert. Ten days later, hunger finally gets to them. John pulls down his pants and says, "I am cutting my dick off so that I will have something to eat." "Think about your sexy wife," says Mike. "Why the hell should I think about my wife?" blasts John. "Well, I thought we might have enough meat for two if you thought about your wife," replies Mike.

Kids say the funniest things

The teacher asked her students to use the word 'fascinate' in a sentence. Mary said, "My family and I went to London Zoo, and we saw all the animals. It was really fascinating."

The teacher said, "That was good, but I wanted the word 'fascinate'."

Sally raised her hand and said, "My family went to Chester Zoo and saw the animals. I was fascinated."

The teacher said, "Good, but I wanted the word 'fascinate'."

Little Johnny raised his hand. The teacher hesitated because Johnny was noted for his bad language. She finally decided there was no way he could damage the word 'fascinate' so she called on him.

Johnny said, "My sister has a sweater with ten buttons, but her tits are so massive she can only fasten eight."

You might think life is rubbish, but imagine being an egg.
You only get smashed once, you only get laid once and the only bird to sit on your face is your mother!

A worthy cause

A driver was stuck in a traffic jam. Suddenly, a man knocked on his window. The driver rolled down his window and asked, “What’s up?” The man said excitedly, “President Bush has been kidnapped by terrorists. They will cover him in petrol and burn him if they don’t get $10million ransom.” The driver asked, “And what do you want me to do?” “Well, we’re going from car to car and collecting for the cause,” answered the man. “Aha... And how much are people giving?” asked the driver. “Oh, somewhere around one or two gallons.”

Contain your excitement

A woman walks into a Mercedes dealership. She browses around, then spots the perfect car and walks over to inspect it. As she bends to feel the fine leather upholstery, a loud fart escapes. Very embarrassed, she looks around nervously to see if anyone has noticed her little accident and hopes a salesperson doesn’t pop up right then. As she turns around, standing next to her is a salesman. “Good day, Madam. How may we help you today?” Very uncomfortably she asks, “Sir, what is the price of this lovely vehicle?” He answers, “Madam, if you farted just touching it, you are going to sh*t yourself when I tell you the price.”

Two can play that game

Little Johnny and his grandfather have gone fishing. After a while, Grandpa gets thirsty and opens up his cooler for some beer. Little Johnny asks, "Grandpa, can I have some beer, too?" "Can you stick your penis in your arsehole?" Grandpa asks back. "No." "Well, then you're not big enough." Grandpa then takes out a cigarette and lights up. Little Johnny sees this and asks for a cigarette. "Can you stick your penis in your arsehole?" Grandpa asks again. "No." "Well, then you're not big enough." Little Johnny gets upset and pulls out some cookies. His grandfather says, "Hey, those cookies look good. Can I have some?" Little Johnny asks, "Can you stick your penis in your arsehole?" Grandpa looks at Johnny and senses his trick so he says, "Well, of course I can, I'm big enough." Little Johnny then says, "Well, go shag yourself, these are my cookies."

A man goes to the doctor and says, "Doctor, I'm having some trouble with my hearing." "What are the symptoms?" asks the doctor. The man replies, "A yellow TV cartoon family."

Speak up

Sarah hated Sunday School and always daydreamed. At school the teacher asks Sarah, "Who made the earth?" Will, who sits behind her, pokes her with a ruler to wake her up. "God Almighty!" she shouts. "Correct," says the teacher. "Who is the saviour of the earth?" asks the teacher. Will poked her again. "Jesus Christ!" she shouts. "Correct. And what did Eve say to Adam after their tenth child?" Will prangs her again and she shouts, "If you poke me with that one more time I'll snap it in half!"

Two cows are standing next to each other in a field. Daisy says to Dolly, "I was artificially inseminated this morning."
"I don't believe you," says Dolly.
"It's true, no bull!"

Last respects

Two guys are golfing on a course that is right next to a cemetery. After they tee off, one of the golfers notices that there is a funeral procession sombrely passing by. He takes off his hat, and places it over his heart. When the funeral is over, the other golfer asks, "Why did you do that?" The man replies, "Well, we were married for almost 40 years. It's the least I could do."

Who's the daddy?

Young Johnny was having nightmares, so his father, Dave, runs into his bedroom to wake him up. "Johnny, what's wrong?" Dave asks. "I dreamt that Auntie Sue had died," the boy replies. The father reassures him that his favourite aunt is perfectly fine, but the next day, coincidentally, Aunt Sue dies. That night, Johnny has another dream – this time that his grandfather was dead. As before, Dave enters his room to wake him up. Dave again reassures him that Grandpa is fine, but on his way home, the boy's grandad is tragically run over by a bus.

The next day, Johnny has another dream – just like before, the father asks what's wrong. This time, Johnny sobs, "I dreamt that my daddy had died."

So, the next day, Dave drives to work very slowly to avoid any accidents, eats nothing for fear of food poisoning and spends the whole day under his desk in case the roof caves in. When he gets home, his wife says to him, "You wouldn't believe the day I had – the milkman didn't come..."

Horse sense

On a farm lived a chicken and a horse, who loved playing together. One day, the horse fell into a bog and began to sink. So off the chicken ran to get help. Running around, he spied the farmer's new Harley motorbike. Finding the keys in the ignition, the chicken sped off with some rope, hoping he had time to save his friend's life. After tying one end to the rear of the bike, the chicken drove forward and, with the aid of the powerful bike, rescued the horse.

A few weeks later, the chicken fell into a mud pit and, soon, he too began to sink. The chicken cried out to the horse to save his life. The horse thought a moment, walked over and straddled the large puddle. He told the chicken to grab his 'thing' and he would lift him out. The chicken got a good grip with its beak and the horse pulled him up and out, saving his life. The moral of the story? When you're hung like a horse, you don't need a Harley to pick up chicks.

Patient: "Doctor, I've got a strawberry stuck up my bum."
Doctor: "I've got some cream for that."

A man's best friend

Howard comes home one evening to find his wife crying.

"What's the matter, darling?" he asks.

"I don't know what to do," she says. "I'd prepared a meal for a special night in, but the dog ate it."

"Don't worry, dear," he says. "I'll get us another dog."

That certain something

A young primary school teacher decides to teach her class a new word. She tells the class about her idea and asks if anyone can tell her a sentence using the word "definitely". Little Sophie's hand shoots up confidently and she says: "The sky is definitely blue." "No, Sophie," says the teacher. "The sky is not definitely blue, it can be grey and cloudy. Anyone else?" Callum's hand pops straight up and he proclaims: "The water is definitely clear." To which the teacher answers: "No, it's not, it can be blue or green." Then Craig, the shyest boy in the class, nervously raises his hand and asks: "If I fart, should it be lumpy?" "No," the teacher responds. So Craig says: "Then I've definitely crapped myself."

Why did the leprechaun wear two condoms?
Ahh, to be sure, to be sure.

Girl talk

A little girl is in line to see Santa. When it's her turn, she climbs up on Santa's lap. Santa asks, "What would you like Santa to bring you for Christmas?" The little girl replies, "I want a Barbie and an Action Man." Santa looks at the little girl for a moment and says, "I think Barbie comes with Ken." "No," says the little girl. "She comes with Action Man – she fakes it with Ken."

How can you tell if you are at a redneck wedding?
Everyone sits on the same side of the church.

I have foreseen it

A worker rings up work and speaks to his boss: "Hi, boss, I'm sorry but I'm not going to be able to come in for work today." The boss replies by asking, "What's wrong with you?" "I have a vision problem," explains the lad. "Sounds serious," says his boss. "What seems to be the problem?" "Well," says the worker, "I just don't see myself at work today."

We'll never know

An ugly man walks into his local with a big grin on his face. "Why so happy?" asks the barman.

"Well, you know I live by a railway," replies the ugly man. "On my way home last night I noticed a woman tied to the tracks. I, of course, freed her, took her back to mine and, to cut a long story short, we made love all night."

"You lucky sod!" says the barman. "Was she pretty?"

"Dunno... never found the head!"

Getting the job done

The CIA had an opening for an assassin. After all the interviews and tests, three candidates were left – two men and a woman. For the final test, CIA agents took one man to a door and gave him a gun. "We must know that you'll follow instructions, no matter what. Inside this room is your wife. Kill her." The man said, "I could never do that." The agent said, "Then you're not the man for this job." The same thing happened with the second man. Finally, the woman is given the same instructions to kill her husband. She took the gun and went into the room. Shots were heard. Then screaming and banging on the walls. Then silence. Then the woman comes out, wiping sweat from her brow. "This gun was loaded with blanks," she said. "I had to beat him to death with the chair."

Why are women like hurricanes?
Because when they arrive they're warm, wet and wild, and when they go they take the house, the car... the whole fking lot.**

The long arm of the law

The SAS, the Parachute Regiment and the Police go on a survival weekend to see who's the best. After basic exercises, the trainer sets them their next task – to catch a rabbit for supper.

First up, the SAS. Infrared goggles on, they drop to the ground and crawl into the woods. They emerge with a rabbit shot clean between the eyes. "Excellent," says the trainer. Next up, the Paras. They finish their cans of lager, smear on camouflage cream and go. They eventually emerge with the charred remains of a rabbit. "A bit messy, but well done," says the trainer.

Lastly, in go the Police, walking slowly, hands behind backs. After an eternity they emerge with a squirrel in handcuffs. "Are you taking the mickey?" asks the trainer. The police team leader nudges the squirrel, who squeaks: "Alright! Alright! I'm a friggin' rabbit!"

Pulling the wool over your eyes

A ventriloquist is visiting New Zealand when he stumbles across a small village and decides to have some fun. Approaching a man on his porch patting his dog, he says, "Can I talk to your dog?" The villager just laughs at him and says, "Are you stupid? The dog doesn't talk." "Are you sure?" asks the ventriloquist. Turning to the dog, he says: "Hello, mate, how's it going?" "I'm doin' all right," the dog replies. At this, the villager looks shocked. "Is this your owner?" "Yep," says the dog. "How does he treat you?" asks the ventriloquist. "Really well. He walks me twice a day, feeds me great food and takes me to the lake once a week to play." "Mind if I talk to your horse?" the ventriloquist asks the villager. The horse tells the ventriloquist that he is also treated pretty well. "I am ridden regularly, brushed down often and kept in a nice barn." "Mind if I talk to your sheep?" the ventriloquist then asks. In a panic, the villager turns around and shouts: "The sheep's a liar!"

Why do women love men who have been circumcised?
They can't resist something with 20 per cent off!

An Englishman, an Irishman, a Scotsman, a Catholic, a Jew and a blind man walk into a pub. The landlord says: "Is this some kind of joke?"

Too good to be true

A man sinks his boat and ends up on a desert island. After about two hours, a beautiful blonde in a tight black leather catsuit walks up the beach. "Would you like a cigarette?" asks the blonde. "Yes, please," replies the shipwrecked man. With that, the blonde unbuttons her left breast pocket seductively and pulls out a packet of cigarettes and a lighter. The blonde then asks, "Would you like a drink?" "Yes, please," replies the man. With that, the blonde unbuttons her right breast pocket seductively and pulls out a large bottle of whiskey and a large bottle of brandy. The blonde then asks the man if he'd like to play around. The man looks surprised and replies, "Don't tell me you have a set of golf clubs in there as well."

**Two rats in a sewer talking to each other. One says to the other, "I'm sick of eating sh*t."
The other rat says, "It's OK, I've spoken to the lads – we're on the p*ss tomorrow."**

Boys will be boys

Two bored casino workers are working at the craps table. An attractive blonde woman arrives and bets $20,000 on a single roll of the dice. She says, "I hope you don't mind, but I feel much luckier when I'm completely nude." With that, she strips from the neck down, rolls the dice and yells, "Come on, baby, mama needs new clothes!" As the dice come to a stop, she jumps up and down and squeals... "Yes! Yes! I won! I won!" She hugs each of the dealers, then picks up her winnings and her clothes and quickly departs. The dealers stare at each other, dumbfounded. Finally, one of them asks, "What did she roll?" The other answers, "I don't know – I thought you were watching." Moral: not all blondes are dumb, but all men are men.

Bird of pray

A priest walks into a pet shop to buy a bird. The owner beckons him over to a parrot. "This is a special parrot," he says. "If you pull the string on the left leg he recites The Lord's Prayer. Pull the string on his right leg and he recites Genesis." "What if you pull both strings?" asks the priest. The parrot screams: "Then I fall off my perch, you idiot!"

Keep on running

A man was ordered by his doctor to lose 75lb due to serious health risks. Desperate, he signs up for a guaranteed weight loss programme. The next day a voluptuous 19-year-old girl arrives, dressed in nothing but running shoes and a sign round her neck, which reads, "If you can catch me, you can have me!" He chases her and after catching up, has his way with her. After a few days of this, he is delighted to find he has lost weight and orders a harder programme. The next day, an even sexier woman turns up, wearing nothing but running shoes and the same sign. After five days of her, he decides to go for the company's hardest programme. "Are you sure?" asks the representative on the phone. "This is our most rigorous programme." "Absolutely," he replies. The next day there's a knock at the door and standing there is a muscular guy wearing nothing but pink running shoes and a sign around his neck that reads, "If I catch you, you're mine."

Did you hear about the man who fell into the machine at the upholsterer's factory?
He's fully recovered.

My mum said never marry a tennis player.
Love means nothing to them.

Grave situation

A man comes home from work to find his dog with the neighbour's pet rabbit in his mouth. The rabbit is dead and the man panics. He thinks the neighbours are going to hate him, so he takes the dirty, chewed-up rabbit into the house, gives it a bath, blow-dries its fur and puts it back into the neighbour's cage, hoping they'll think it died of natural causes. A few days later, the neighbour asks the guy, "Did you hear that Fluffy died?" The man stammers and says, "Um, no. What happened?" The neighbour replies, "We just found him dead in his cage one day, but the weird thing is that the day after we buried him, we went outside and someone had dug him up, given him a bath and put him back into the cage. There must be some really sick people out there!"

A dyslexic goth sold his soul to Santa.
A dyslexic rock star choked on his own Vimto.
A dyslexic went to a toga party... as a goat.

Wife support

A woman accompanied her husband to the doctor's office. After his check-up, the doctor called the wife into his office alone. He said, "Your husband is suffering from a very severe disease, combined with horrible stress. If you don't do the following, your husband will surely die. Each morning, fix him a healthy breakfast. Be pleasant, and make sure he is in a good mood. For lunch, make him a nutritious meal. Don't burden him with chores, as he will have had a hard day. Don't discuss your problems with him, it will only make his stress worse. And most importantly... make love with your husband several times a week. If you can do this for the next ten months to a year, I think your husband will regain his health completely." On the way home, the husband asked his wife, "What did the doctor say?" "You're going to die," she replied.

Never look a gift horse in the mouth

A cop on horseback is at some traffic lights, and next to him is a kid on his bike. The cop says to the kid, "Nice bike you got there. Santa bring that for you?" The kid says, "Yeah." The cop says, "Tell Santa next year to put a back light on that bike." The kid says, "Nice horse you got there. Did Santa bring that for you?" The cop replies, "Yeah." The kid says, "Well, tell Santa next year to put the dick underneath the horse, instead of on top."

Money well spent

Two men standing in a bar have been drinking all day long. Both are heavily inebriated. The first man goes a bit green, then throws up all over himself. "Oh no, the wife's going to kill me; I promised I wouldn't drink today." His friend stops him short: "Don't you worry about a thing, pal. Place a ten-pound note in your jacket pocket and tell the missus some other guy hurled on you. Then the man put that money in your pocket to pay for the cleaning bill." The guy agrees and spends the rest of the day downing beers. On arriving home, his wife sees the mess he's in straight away and she asks: "Have you been drinking?" "No, I certainly have not. Some other guy threw up on me and gave me a tenner for my troubles. Check in my jacket pocket if you don't believe me." She checks. "But there's £20 in here." "Oh yeah, didn't I say? He sh*t my pants as well..."

Why do housewives love Arsenal so much?
Because they stay on top for so long, but always come second.

Serving time

A woman awakens during the night to find that her husband is not in bed. She puts on her robe and goes downstairs to look for him. She finds him sitting at the kitchen table with a cup of coffee in front of him. He appears to be in deep thought, just staring at the wall. She watches as he wipes a tear from his eye and takes a sip of his coffee.

"What's the matter, dear?" she asks tenderly. "Why are you down here at this time of night?" The husband looks up. "Do you remember when we were first dating, we were so young?" he asks. "Yes, I do," she replies.

The husband continues, his voice brimming with emotion. "Do you remember when your father caught us in the back seat of my car making love?" "Yes, I remember," says the wife.

The husband continues. "Do you remember when he shoved the shotgun in my face and said, 'Either you marry my daughter, or I'll see that you go to jail for 30 years'?"

"I remember that," she replies softly, taking his hand. He wipes a tear from his cheek and says, "I would have got out today."

Somebody complimented me on my driving the other day. They left me a note on my windscreen saying, "Parking Fine." So that was nice.

Not as stupid as she looks

A blonde walks into a bank in London and asks to see the manager. She says she's going to Hong Kong on business for two weeks and needs to borrow £5,000. The manager says the bank will need some kind of security for the loan, so the blonde hands over the keys to a new Ferrari. The car is parked on the street in front of the bank, she has the title and everything checks out. The manager and the tellers all enjoy a good laugh at the blonde and an employee of the bank then drives the Ferrari into the bank's underground garage and parks it there. Two weeks later, the blonde returns, repays the £5,000 and the interest, which comes to £15.41. The manager says, "While you were away, madam, we checked your details and discovered you're a millionairess. What puzzles us is, why would you bother to borrow £5,000?" The blonde replies, "Where else in London can I park my car for two weeks for only £15.41 and expect it to be there when I come back?"

Man says to God, "God, why did you make woman so beautiful?"
God says, "So you would love her."
"But, God," the man arrogantly asks, "why did you make her so dumb?"
God says, "So she would love you."

Scared stiff

A taxi passenger tapped the driver on the shoulder to ask him a question. The driver screamed, lost control of the car and stopped just centimetres from a shop window. The driver turned round and said, “Look, mate, don’t do that again. You scared the daylights out of me!” The passenger apologised and said he didn’t realise that a tap on the shoulder could scare the driver so much. The driver replied, “Sorry, it’s not your fault, mate. Today is my first day as a cab driver – I’ve been driving hearses for the last 25 years.”

A golfer was lining up his tee shot.
“What’s taking so long?” demanded his partner.
“My wife is watching me from the club house. This needs to be a perfect shot.”
“Forget it,” said his partner, “you’ll never hit her from here.”

Sign of the times

A guy walks into a pub and orders a drink. After a few more, he needs to go to the toilet. He doesn’t want anyone to steal his drink so he puts a sign on it saying, “I spat in this beer, do not drink!” After a few minutes, he returns and there’s another sign next to his beer saying, “So did I!”

Here we go gathering nuts in May

Alan and his friend Martin went out hunting. Martin had never hunted before, so he was following Alan's lead. Alan saw a herd of deer and told Martin to stay in the exact spot he was and to be quiet. A moment later, Alan heard a scream. He ran back and asked Martin what had happened. "A snake slithered across my feet," said Martin, "but that didn't make me scream. Then a bear came up to me and snarled, but I still didn't scream."

"So why did you?" Alan asked, infuriated.

"Well," Martin went on, "two squirrels crawled up my trousers and I heard one of them say, 'Should we take 'em home or eat 'em now?'"

Caught short

Two women walking home drunk need to pee, so they duck into a graveyard. They have no bog roll, so one woman uses her pants and throws them away. The other uses a ribbon from a wreath. The next day their husbands are talking. "We'd better keep an eye on our wives," says one man. "Mine came home without her knickers." "You think that's bad," says the other man. "Mine had a card up her bum saying, 'From all the lads at the fire station, we'll never forget you.'"

A husband says to his wife: "I'm off down the pub. Get your coat on."
The wife says: "Why? Am I coming with you?"
He replies: "No, I'm switching the heating off."

Birthday blues

Two weeks ago was my 45th birthday. I wasn't feeling too good that morning, but as I walked into my office, my secretary Janet said, "Good morning, boss. Happy birthday." And I felt a little better that someone had remembered. I worked until noon, then Janet knocked on my door and said, "You know, it's such a beautiful day outside, and it's your birthday, let's go to lunch, just you and me." We went to lunch. On the way back to the office, she said, "You know, it's such a beautiful day. Let's go to my apartment." After arriving at her apartment she said, "Boss, if you don't mind, I think I'll go into the bedroom and slip into something more comfortable." "Sure!" I excitedly replied. She went into the bedroom and, in a few minutes, returned carrying a huge birthday cake – followed by my wife, children and dozens of our friends, all singing Happy Birthday. And I just sat there – on the couch – naked.

Three tough mice

Three mice were sitting at a bar talking about how tough they were. The first mouse slams a shot and says, “I play with mousetraps for fun. I’ll run into one on purpose and as it’s closing on me, I’ll grab the bar and bench press it 20 to 30 times.” The second mouse turns to him, slams a shot and says, “That’s nothing. I take those poison bait tablets, cut them up and snort them, just for the fun of it.” The third mouse turns to both of them, slams a shot, gets up and walks away and shouts, “I’m going home to shag the cat.”

Hidden talents

Two buddies are sitting in a singles’ club and talking about another guy sitting at the other end of the bar. “I don’t get it,” complained the first guy. “He’s not good-looking, he has no taste in clothes, drives a beat-up wreck of a car, yet he always manages to go home with the most beautiful women here!”

“Yeah,” replies his buddy. “He’s not even very good conversationally – all he does is sit there and lick his eyebrows.”

I'm alright!

A young couple visit a marriage counsellor. The counsellor asks the wife what the problem is. She responds, "My husband suffers from premature ejaculation." The counsellor turns to her husband and enquires, "Is that true?" The husband replies, "Well, not exactly – it's her that suffers, not me."

A small boy is lost, so he goes up to a policeman and says, "I can't find my dad."
"What's he like?" the policeman enquires.
"Beer and women," replies the boy.

Third-rate performance

A woman meets a smart man in a bar. They talk and end up leaving together. Back at his flat, she notices his bedroom is packed with small teddy bears lined up all the way along the floor, medium-sized ones on a shelf a little higher, and enormous fluffy bears on the top shelf along the wall. The woman is surprised, but decides not to mention it as she is quite impressed by the man's sensitive side. After an intense night of passion, the woman rolls over and asks, "Tell me, how was it?" The man replies: "Help yourself to any prize from the bottom shelf, love."

Your number's up

Five Germans in an Audi Quattro arrive at the Italian border. The Italian Customs agent stops them: "It'sa illegala to putta five people in a Quattro."

"Wat do you mean it'z illegal?" asks the German driver.

"Quattro meansa four," replies the Italian official.

"Quattro is just ze name of ze automobile," the German says in disbelief. "Look at ze papers. This car is designed to kerry five."

"You can'ta pulla thata one on me!" replies the Italian. "Quattro meansa four. You hava five people ina your car and you are breakinga tha law!"

The German driver is angry. "You idiot! Call ze supervisor over, I want to speak to somevone with more intelligence!"

"Sorry," says the Italian. "He'sa busy with two guys in a Fiat Uno."

Two buckets of sick are walking down the street. One bursts into tears.
"What's the matter?" asks the other.
He replies: "This is where I was brought up."

Now that you've enjoyed *Nuts Joke Book*, look out for these other great *Nuts* books in your local bookshop!

Nuts Pub Ammo

Hundreds of great facts from the UK's most popular men's magazine

Price: £4.99

ISBN: 1-84442-135-X

The Big Book of Nuts

Women, cars, facts, jokes and more in this brilliant full-colour hardback book

Price: £9.99

ISBN: 1-84442-143-5

Save money and get *Nuts* magazine delivered to your door every week

Subscribe to *Nuts* today!

Go to: www.nuts.co.uk/intbj

or call: 0845 676 7778 quoting code 23b